Delay Learning in Artificial
Neural Networks

CHAPMAN & HALL NEURAL COMPUTING SERIES

Series editors: Igor Aleksander, Imperial College, London
Richard Mammone, Rutgers University, New Jersey, USA

Since the beginning of the current revival of interest in Neural Networks, the subject is reaching considerable maturity, while at the same time becoming of interest to people working in an increasing number of disciplines. This series seeks to address some of the specializations that are developing through the contributions of authoritative writers in the field. This series will address both specializations and applications of neural computing techniques to particular areas.

1. **Delay Learning in Artificial Neural Networks**
   Catherine Myers
2. **Neural Network VLSI**
   Alan Murray and Lionel Tarassenko
3. **Hybrid Artificial Intelligence Systems**
   Peter Churcher
4. **Neurons and Symbols**
   Igor Aleksander and Helen Morton
5. **Speech Recognition**
   The role of neural networks
   E. Ambikairajah with contributions from E. Jones

Delay Learning
in Artificial
Neural Networks

Catherine E. Myers

Center for Molecular and Behavioural Neuroscience,
Rutgers University, Newark, USA

CHAPMAN & HALL
London · Glasgow · New York · Tokyo · Melbourne · Madras

**Published by Chapman & Hall, 2-6 Boundary Row, London
SE1 8HN**

Chapman & Hall, 2-6 Boundary Row, London SE1 8HN, UK

Blackie Academic & Professional, Wester Cleddens Road, Bishopbriggs, Glasgow G64 2NZ, UK

Van Nostrand Reinhold Inc., 115 5th Avenue, New York NY10003, USA

Chapman & Hall Japan, Thomson Publishing Japan, Hirakawacho Nemoto Building, 6F, 1-7-11 Hirakawa-cho, Chiyoda-ku, Tokyo 102, Japan

Chapman & Hall Australia, Thomas Nelson Australia, 102 Dodds Street, South Melbourne, Victoria 3205, Australia

Chapman & Hall India, R. Seshadri, 32 Second Main Road, CIT East, Madras 600 035, India

First edition 1992

© 1992 Catherine E. Myers

Typeset in 10/12 Times by Thomson Press (India) Ltd., New Delhi
Printed in Great Britain by T. J. Press (Padstow) Ltd., Padstow, Cornwall

ISBN 0 412 45050 X   0 442 31627 5(USA)

A catalogue record for this book is available from the British Library

Library of Congress Cataloging-in-Publication data

Myers, Catherine.
    Delay learning in artificial neural networks / Catherine Myers.
        p.   cm.—(Chapman & Hall neural computing)
    Based on the author's thesis (Ph.D.—Imperial College, London).
    Includes bibliographical references (p.   ) and index.
    ISBN 0-442-31627-5
    1. Neural networks (Computer science)   I. Title. II. Series.
QA76.87.M94   1992
006.3′1—dc20   92-19237
                                                              CIP

⊗ Printed on permanent acid-free text paper, manufactured in accordance with the proposed ANSI/NISO Z 39.48-199X and ANSI Z 39.48-1984

To
Russell Myers,
who didn't quite see this.
May he have found his heaven.

Contents

Preface

> One thing that connectionist networks have in common with
> brains is that if you open them up and peer inside, all you can
> see is a big pile of goo.
>
> Michael Moser and Paul Smolensky (1989)

One way of dichotomizing the field of artificial neural network research is into research devoted to producing fast, intelligent and/or adaptive machines as opposed to research devoted to producing ever more accurate models of learning processes in the organic brain. The first school is usually peopled by engineers and the second by cognitive scientists. Often, the two schools are necessarily at odds. Given a particular problem, the engineer tends to opt for the solution which is most likely to perform well, given current technology and theory. The cognitive scientist may not care if the mechanisms actually work – or produce useable machines – so long as the result in some sense resembles the brain.

Certainly, both approaches to research are productive. It is becoming apparent, though, that there is also insight to be gained from the middle ground: where the study of the brain may provide insight into a practical method for achieving some result. Researchers in this third branch of neural network research proceed by investigating solutions to a particular problem which are constrained by data from the brain but which must be useful from a pragmatic end view.

The topic of this book is an approach to solving the problem of delay learning by machine. This is a cognitive problem which is higher-level than many neural networks can address, but which is nowhere near so high-level as, for instance, language understanding. It is also a problem which even fairly simple animals can solve to some extent, but for which there are no satisfactory solutions in machine learning yet.

Two chapters of this book are dedicated to explaining this approach, termed attention-driven buffering, and to providing examples of pattern recognition to which the technique can usefully be applied.

However, given that there is something to be gained from keeping an eye on how living systems solve learning problems, two chapters are also devoted to examining the performance of this technique on problems meant to mimic real learning situations in lower animals – specifically in an octopus, one of the 'highest' of the invertebrates. As it turns out, the technique is suitable for operant conditioning problems like those the octopus and all higher animals can solve, and there are also some grounds for believing that the octopus, and even mammals, may be using similar approaches to delay learning.

In the long term, the study of artificial neural networks will be able to contribute back to both engineering and cognitive science. It should provide the engineers with machines which can achieve results that cannot be achieved easily with any other methodology. It should also provide the cognitive scientists first with constructive proofs that their learning models actually can achieve the desired kinds of learning, and more interestingly, with predictions. The cognitive scientists can then use these predictions to discriminate between models by comparing with the actual results in animals.

This last is critically important, but has long been mostly ignored by neural network researchers. Instead, the tendency has been to take a model of some facet of learning, implement it in a neural network simulation, and pronounce 'Q.E.D' – but of course the successful operation of such a simulation (gratifying as it is for the programmer) does not actually prove anything. The real value of such simulations becomes apparent after this stage – when a new experiment is proposed, and the workings of the simulation and experimental animals can be properly compared.

In writing this book, I have tried to satisfy both the engineer and cognitive scientist, even though their demands may conflict. This is why the book divides into two logical halves: one dedicated to showing that the delay learning technique proposed is a useful addition to the machine builder's toolkit, and one dedicated to showing correspondence between the technique and animal learning data. I hope that readers from both schools of neural network research will find it worth their while to read both sections. I have not assumed any particular knowledge on the part of the reader, but I expect that readers generally will have some experience with artificial neural networks, and the book is meant to expand on a small and specific region of the field rather than to provide an introduction to or justification of the field.

The one significant exception to this philosophy occurs in Chapter 3. The neural model I use, the probabilistic logic node (PLN), will perhaps be unfamiliar to readers for whom neural network research implies use of the error backpropagation learning algorithm. For this reason, a full account of the PLN model seemed justified. However, it must be stressed that the delay learning technique described in this book is essentially independent of the node model used.

This book is based on my PhD thesis, completed at Imperial College London, and dealing with the same topics. During my stay at Imperial, I was supervised by Prof Igor Aleksander. Both my thesis and this book owe immense debts to his patience, encouragement, knowledge and inexhaustible good humour during this period. Also during my stay, the Neural Systems group he heads has expanded from a few students vaguely interested in the newly reborn field of neural networks into a full team of enthusiastic researchers. The group has provided me with personal support and technical experts in many areas, and much of what I know and what surfaces in this book was introduced to me by one of them or suggested itself during many discussions and seminars. They have also been great friends, and my thanks go to them all, including Stephen Bridge, Felipe Franca, Eamon Fulcher, Mike Gera, Teresa Ludermir, James Lucy, Janko Mrsic-Flogel, Panayotis Ntourntoufis, Adrian Redgers, Nick Sales, Phillipe de Wilde, and all the others who have passed through. I am also hugely indebted to Lee Flanagan, especially for always knowing what to do during the endless stream of minor crises of the past few years. Finally, my thanks to those who have provided me with useful comments and criticisms on my research, most especially Antonia Jones, Denise Gorse, John Taylor, J. Z. Young, Jurgen Schmidhuber, David Martland and Michael Wong.

My PhD research was funded by a National Science Foundation (USA) Graduate Fellowship; this book was mostly written while I was funded by the ESRC/Medical Research Council/SERC Joint Cognitive Science/Human-Computer Interface Initiative and by the Japanese Human Frontiers in Science Program.

Catherine Myers.

1

Introduction

Why is man different from the animals? What is consciousness, how does it arise, and is it only man who possesses it? Does each human being have a soul, distinct from the material body? Is the mind something that arises from the brain, or is it something altogether separate?

In a sense, all of these questions ask the same thing: how does the brain work? If we knew exactly how the brain worked, down to the level of the smallest brain cell and up to the level of interplay between huge areas of it, we could point to the abilities of man which animals do not possess. We could point to the group of cells (or the properties of them) which give rise to consciousness; or failing that, we could at least conclude that it is not a property of the brain *per se*. And we could use the knowledge of brains to build machines which, even if they were not meant to imitate humans, might at least be as clever as animals – which in turn are much better than any modern computer at processing sensory data, learning the implications of the data, and adjusting behaviour to survive in an ever-changing world.

The problem of course is that we are a long, long way from understanding how the brain works. It is even possible that we can never know – that we can never understand brains while we are using brains themselves to do the learning. But this is perhaps unduly pessimistic. We are beginning to understand how individual brain cells (neurons) work; we are beginning to understand the functions of groups of neurons in the brain; and we are beginning to understand how information is stored and retrieved using regions of millions of neurons.

There has been another development, which has its roots throughout the past few decades, but which has taken on especial momentum within the past twenty years: the use of computer modelling of the brain and of learning. At one extreme lies artificial neural network (or parallel distributed processing or connectionist) research. This involves the simulation of units which are more or less like neurons, and which can then be built into networks or 'miniature brains'. Sometimes it is useful to build elaborate detail into these units, and by watching their interactions to test theories on how individual neurons in the brain behave. At other times, each unit can be simplified drastically, if the experimenter is more interested in watching how a network of these units can come to store information or learn appropriate responses to environmental inputs.

The other extreme is symbolic processing, which is usually what is meant by the term artificial intelligence (AI). The emphasis here is not on the implementation in terms of neuron-like units, but on how symbols can be manipulated to give intelligent-seeming behaviour. An AI system might, for example, consist of a collection of rules about how to diagnose malfunction of a car. The system might include rules like: "If the car always veers to the right and if the tyres are all properly inflated and if the steering column is intact, then the problem is probably a misaligned axle." These rules might be programmed in at the start by a human expert, or the system might be required to learn these rules by experience with test cases.

With these techniques, together with the vast and ever-increasing store of data from those studying living brains in animals and humans, it is possible to build some models of how it is that brains can accomplish some of their astounding tasks. This is interesting for its own sake, and for the answers to some of those questions listed above, and also for the sake of knowledge of how we can repair the brain when it goes wrong. It also can provide insight into how to build machines which are, if not intelligent, at least more capable of functioning in an intelligent-seeming way. For today's machines are nothing like as sophisticated as very simple animals in a variety of ways.

The word processor on my desk and the larger computer I use to run experiments are both terrific at additions and multiplications, and can do arithmetic much faster – and more accurately – than I can. They are also very good at following orders, in the shape of programs. But let me misspell one word in that program, or make one logical error, and the computer will either fail to run altogether or else produce an answer which is altogether different from what I intended. On the other hand, if I were to misspell one word in this paragraph, the more pedantic readers would recognize the mistake, but even they would not fail to grasp the meaning of the words. Similarly, if someone I have known from childhood lets his beard grow or colours her hair, I will not fail to recognize them on that account. Yet the majority of conventional computer programs which execute image recognition could not deal with that sort of facial distortion.

And it gets worse than this. There are a variety of methods available for providing the computer with the ability to learn. Connectionist models deal with this especially, but there are plenty of very sophisticated adaptive rule-based approaches as well. The way these paradigms usually work is something like this: "Accept an input, and produce an output according to your current knowledge. If the output is right, adjust your internal knowledge so that you are more likely to reproduce that output when similar input appears again; if the output is wrong, adjust your knowledge so that you are more likely to produce the correct output instead. Carry on in this way until you consistently produce the correct outputs to all inputs." The problem is that learning in the real world is almost never this neatly codified.

One problem is that an animal doesn't sit quietly while the world produces input patterns for it to practice responding to. An animal is constantly acting and exploring, and the sensory input it receives depends on what it has just done. The taste of food is experienced only after the animal has placed something in its mouth; it can do that only after it has approached and grasped the object with limbs or teeth or whatever is appropriate. And it will only be able to approach an object if it has roamed around enough to encounter the object in the first place. Animal learning is **exploratory**: what an animal receives as input to its sensors depends on the environment in which it finds itself as a result (at least partially) of its own actions.

The next problem is that when the animal produces an output (i.e., acts), the world does not tell it what the 'correct, optimal' output would have been. The information from the environment is more likely to come in the form of **reinforcement**: taste or other positive signals to encourage the action, or pain or other negative signals to discourage it. But if the reinforcement is negative, it doesn't tell the animal what action should be learned in place of the current one, just that the current one is unsuitable.

Finally, and most difficult of all, is that reinforcement does not tend to come at every instant, after each action (or failure to act) occurs. An animal spots a foodstuff, decides to investigate, approaches and grasps it, places it in the mouth – and only then does the reinforcing sensation of taste begin. Yet what must be reinforced in the first place is the decision to eat which was undertaken some time ago, back when the animal first spotted the food. This means that the animal must be capable of storing the original input, the vision of food at a distance, until the reinforcement arrives. To complicate matters, it is possible that other unrelated reinforcements arrive in the meantime. If on the way to the food, the animal hits its paw against a rock, the pain will arrive before the positive reinforcement of taste. Somehow the animal must skip over the negative reinforcement as irrelevant and come to associate the positive reinforcement with the sight of distant food if it is to learn correctly. This problem is known as **delay learning**: learning the correct output to an input, even if the reinforcement associated with that input does not arrive immediately, and even if other, unrelated reinforcements arrive during the delay.

These three ideas, exploratory learning, reinforcement learning and especially delay learning, are central themes explored in this book. They are important in that animals successfully cope with them, and so we would like machines to be able to cope with them also. But they are also necessary for some very non-biological tasks to which learning machines can be applied: for example, a machine which learns to play chess will have inputs which depend upon its own last moves, will not be told what the optimal move was, only whether it's doing well overall, and will often not receive reinforcement information until the end of a game.

This book considers first several examples of learning machines based on artificial neural networks which accomplish at least one of exploratory, reinforcement or delay learning. Some are extremely elegant within their domain, but none specifically satisfies all three criteria fully as they are defined here. The purpose of this book is to describe a type of learning machine which does.

The next step is to describe and analyse a class of machines which allow for exploratory, reinforcement and delay learning. Through a method called attention-driven buffering, systems can satisfy these three criteria in a way that none of the previously described approaches can, yet they represent a compromise between many of these earlier ideas. The machines which result can be applied to theoretical or to game-playing problems. What would be more interesting would be to compare them with the situations which face an animal foraging in the wild.

Unfortunately, the brain of an animal such as a small mammal is too large and too poorly understood to allow a computer system to make a very convincing claim of modelling it. However, setting the sights on something a little less grand, there are animals which are capable of learning arbitrary associations but with much smaller (and rather better understood) brains. One such is the common octopus. By any account, the octopus ranks far below humans and other 'intelligent' animals on an evolutionary scale; yet the octopus can accomplish vision and learning tasks which a programmer would be proud to achieve on a computer. What is interesting here is that the octopus can be trained to attack one object and to reject another, which is very much the same sort of behaviour – conditioned learning – as can be seen in higher animals up to and including humans. But the octopus has a much smaller brain, one which has been well-studied by zoologists, and therefore one which can be modelled to a fair degree of accuracy. The later chapters of this book present a computer model, based on the strategies developed for exploratory, reinforcement, delay learning with performance in conditioning tasks which can be compared to the octopus.

Obviously it is a long way from building a robot which behaves like an octopus to one which behaves like a human being. It is a long way from an octopus even to the least intelligent of mammals. But the octopus is still a lot more sophisticated as a learning machine than any computer to date: the robot has yet to be designed that could cope with the vagaries of life with which the octopus copes daily.

If we can produce a machine which is as successful in a real-world environment as a simple animal, we can expect to have answered some difficult questions about how that animal learns. And in turn we can expect that at least some of that knowledge may scale up to answer questions about human beings, our brains and our minds.

1.1 Definitions of learning and reinforcement

The nature of this field is such that almost any coherent description must begin with some basic definitions. Artificial neural network research has hijacked its name from the biological vocabulary, and currently a 'neural network' can be understood to mean anything ranging from a region of living brain tissue, to a simulation of such a region, to an information processing machine whose units bear no detailed resemblance to those forming a living neural network. For clarity, the phrase **neural network** will be used in this book to refer to networks found within machines or computer simulations, while 'brain' or 'biological neural network' will refer to the sort found in living creatures. Neural networks are composed of 'nodes' or 'units', brains of 'neurons' or 'cells'.

Next, in defining a machine based on a neural network, it is necessary to speak of the machine's *behaviour* with respect to its *environment*, and which changes as a function of *reinforcement* through a process known as *learning*.

These four critical terms are adapted from the vocabulary of psychology, where they are reasonably well-defined. Their use in the context of neural network research is almost metaphorical. Certainly a child learning to speak, or even a rat learning to traverse a maze, are performing dramatically more complex operations than a machine which learns to produce a certain output pattern when another certain pattern is input to it. Yet at an abstract level there is also a fundamental similarity: all three over time increase their likelihood of 'correct' performance in a given situation. The definitions of learning, reinforcement and the rest which are appropriate to neural network research reflect the psychological definitions at this abstract level.

The input and output of a learning system can be thought of as stimulus and response: the former is a contributing cause in the production of the latter. The responses of the system over time constitute its behaviour.

The **environment** within which the system operates provides the system with input and observes its responses. The environment may be a computer program which calculates what the next input should be, or it may be a portion of the real physical world which the system samples with its sensors and influences with its outputs. If such a system receives proprioceptive input detailing the status of its effectors, this is also included under the heading of environmental inputs.

Some of the input to a learning system may be classified as **reinforcement**. A reinforcement is a stimulus which is capable of causing the learning system to adjust its behaviours. In general, a *positive* reinforcement or **reward** arriving after a response should make the system more likely to repeat the same response under similar input conditions in the future. *Negative* reinforcement or **punishment** should make that response less likely in future.

Finally, given these definitions, **learning** is an adaptation of behaviour which tends to maximize positive and/or minimize negative reinforcement from the environment.

1.2 Exploratory learning in a neural network

One way to dichotomize learning is as passive or exploratory. In **passive learning**, the system is shown an input stimulus together with the desired response and possibly also the reinforcement that would be elicited. In **exploratory learning**, under given stimulus conditions, the animal executes a response and receives reinforcement that directs learning.

It is a matter of some debate whether passive learning occurs in animals: Tighe (1982, p. 163) suggests that "the two most fundamental questions in learning theory [are] whether learning can occur without reinforcement and whether learning can occur without response."

There is evidence that passive learning occurs in humans: for example, a student memorizing a list of battles and dates learns associations without really responding and without any reinforcement (except of course the distant goal of passing the exam). In laboratory experiments, children have been shown to learn 'by observation': seeing one behaviour rewarded, they later imitate that behaviour themselves. For example, children shown a movie where an adult attacked a doll and then was given a sweet later (without prompting) behaved more aggressively toward the doll than did children shown a movie in which the same attack was punished by scolding (Fisher, 1980).

It has also been argued that animals can learn associations in the absence of either response or reinforcement, under conditions known as sensory preconditioning. Dogs were first exposed to repeated pairings of tone and light flashes, and then trained to make a response to the tone; later, shown the light flash, they made the same trained response (Tighe, 1982, pp. 129–45). The animals seemed to have learned an association of tone and light in the preconditioning stage, before they were required to make any response. One difficulty in proving this assertion is that just because there was no overtly detectable response in the preconditioning stage does not necessarily mean that no response existed.

It is much easier to cite examples of exploratory learning: in a typical laboratory experiment, the animal is placed in an apparatus containing, for example, a lever. The animal explores its new environment until it happens to push the lever. At this point, a food pellet drops into the food tray. The next time the lever is pressed, the same reward arrives. Soon, the animal learns to press the lever to obtain food. It has not been shown what to do; instead, the animal stumbled across reinforcement by exploring with different behaviours. The (positive) reinforcement encourages it to repeat one particular behaviour, and when the animal consistently does, it has learned to solve the problem.

Using this method, a rat can be trained to run through a maze to reach food, a pigeon can learn to peck at buttons at a certain rate to obtain water, a dog can learn to jump over a barrier to avoid electric shock. One famous rat was trained to climb a spiral path to reach a drawbridge, cross it to reach a ladder to a track across which he propelled a handcart to reach the stairs to a top level; once there, he passed through a transparent tube over a canyon, raised a flag, and lowered himself to the ground floor in a 'dumbwaiter' – at which point he could press a lever to receive a food pellet: the reinforcement for the entire operation (Pierrel and Sherman, 1963). This complex task was learned by chaining simpler operations: the rat first learned that a level press yielded food; then he was taught to lower himself in the dumbwaiter for access to the lever, and so on backwards.

A crucial feature of exploratory learning is that it involves a response which leads to reinforcement. If the animal makes no response, it never receives reinforcement. (Of course, it is sometimes true that to do nothing is also to do something. An animal which executed no response for a long period of time would begin to receive negatively reinforcing hunger signals, indicating that the present behaviour should be altered). The defining characteristics of exploratory learning are that both reinforcement and to a greater or lesser degree subsequent input stimuli depend upon the response behaviour of the animal. In foraging conditions, for example, a motor output response which causes the animal to turn its head to the left results in a reactive slide of visual input on the retina; but at the same time, the visual input may also be altered if other animals are moving within the visual field, or if the scene darkens as a cloud moves across the sun. For this reason – the independent changes in other aspects of the environment – the influence of response output on subsequent input is critical but possibly only partial.

Exploratory learning by machine can be further subdivided into empirical learning and trial-and-error learning.

Empirical learning machines typically have an initial training phase which is off-line: the system operates in simulation mode, and its responses have no real consequence. During the training phase, the machine experiments with various responses and observes the results (in terms of reinforcement, subsequent input, or both). It must then store this knowledge away. After this phase, when the system is actually running, it can reference this body of knowledge, estimate the results of a particular response, and judge whether to make that response.

An example of such a system is MURPHY (Mel, 1988), in which a neural network drives a 3-jointed robot arm and receives its input from a video camera filming the position of that arm (Figure 1.1). White spots are stuck to the arm, so that the thresholded camera output shows only those spots on an otherwise featureless background, and gives a simple picture of arm position.

The neural network consists of two layers of units. The lower layer contains units which each monitor a broad region of the camera output, and are activated when a white spot falls into their region. The regions of neighbouring units overlap, so that a unit whose region centres upon a white spot fires maximally, while its neighbours, monitoring regions which contain less of the spot, will be proportionally less active.

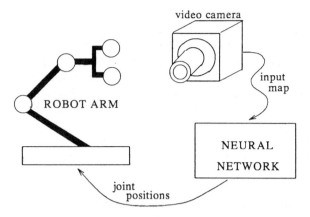

Figure 1.1 *The experimental set-up for MURPHY, an empirical exploratory learning system; a video camera monitors the movements of a robot arm controlled by a neural network.*

The upper layer of units code the angle for each joint of the robot arm. There is a selection of position-encoding units for each joint, of which the one encoding the actual joint angle should be maximally active. Adjustable weights connect units in the two layers.

During training, the arm is moved through a sample set of joint configurations. The neural network 'notes' the patterns of visual feature unit activity and position-encoding feature activity, and adjusts its weights: so that the weight between one visual feature unit and three position-encoding units (one for each joint) is proportional to the probability that that visual unit is strongly active when the joints are in that configuration.

Later, after this training phase, MURPHY's neural network has memorized a body of data correlating visual input patterns with the arm positions that give rise to them. During operation, MURPHY is given a target position for the 'hand' at the tip of the robot arm. MURPHY generates several possible joint positions similar to its current one, and recalls the visual image associated with each. It selects the visual image which represents the hand being closest to target, and generates several possible joint positions from *that* one. After several iterations of this process, MURPHY will have generated a trio of joint angles which result in the hand being located at the target position. It can then simply command the arm to implement those three angles, thereby moving the hand to the target.

What is notable about empirical learning is that it involves no supervision or reinforcement – during training there is no sense that the system has made a 'correct' or 'incorrect' response. The system is merely exploring and recording for later reference. Of course, this very feature requires an off-line (potentially lengthy) training phase before the system is ready for operation, and also requires that the system is unable to damage itself during this experimentation!

There is some evidence that something akin to empirical learning – i.e., learning without reinforcement – occurs in animals. For example, rats allowed to explore a maze without food, and then trained to find food in the goal location learn this faster than rats without prior exploration experience; while rats placed in a maze containing food, but who are not hungry, can later return efficiently to where they saw the food – indicating that they have indeed learned about the maze (Tighe, 1982, pp. 99–123). However, it is hard to eliminate the concept of reinforcement in animal learning; for example, the mere sight of food might be positively reinforcing, even if the animal is satiated.

An alternative form of exploratory learning involves **trial and error**. Here, even during learning there *are* distinct goals; the system tries out responses and notes the success they have in achieving these goals.

One such system is Kuperstein and Rubenstein's INFANT (1989), which has a task similar to MURPHY's. The neural network controls a robot arm with five degrees of freedom (four controlled by the neural net); its goal is to reach for a cylindrical object hanging in three-dimensional space, and its input is a map derived from stereo images provided by twin video cameras.

The neural network consists of four nodes, and their outputs $\theta_1, \theta_2, \theta_3, \theta_4$, specify joint positions. Each node j receives weighted input from all elements x_i in the input map, and computes $\theta_j = \sum w_{ji} x_i$.

During training, a position for the arm is generated randomly – specified by joint angles $\theta_1^*, \theta_2^*, \theta_3^*, \theta_4^*$ – and the arm is moved into that position. The cameras record the resulting image, and this is transformed into an input map. The net then produces θ_j at each node. The error at each node can then be

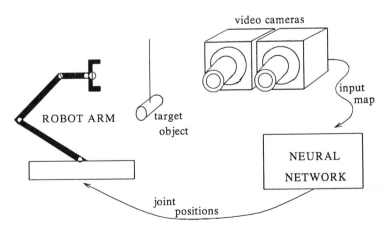

Figure 1.2 *The INFANT system; twin cameras provide a stereo image of a five-dimensional robot arm under neural network control, reaching for a hanging object.*

computed simply as deviation from the actual joint angle: $\varepsilon_j = \theta_j - \theta_j^*$, and the net is trained by adjusting the weight w_{ji} to node j from input i by an amount proportional to its error.

Over many iterations, the system learns to produce the correct output joint specifications for each input map. Then, during operation, the target object is placed at some position in space; an input map is generated, and the system should then produce the output joint specifications which would result in the robot hand being superimposed over the target object.

In a different example of trial and error learning, Barto and Sutton (1981) have designed a system which does not require an off-line training phase. Their system learns as it goes along, and experiences the reinforcements that result from its responses. The task involves mimicking a simple 'organism' which moves through an environment toward a target location (Figure 1.3). The environment contains four landmarks, and these emit odours which decay in strength with distance. The strengths of these odours at the current location serve as input to the organism. The neural network controlling the organism's movement contains four units, each receiving weighted input of each smell, and each outputting an instruction to move north, south, east or west, respectively. The organism moves in the direction specified by the most active unit. (If two non-opposing units, such as north and east, are both strongly

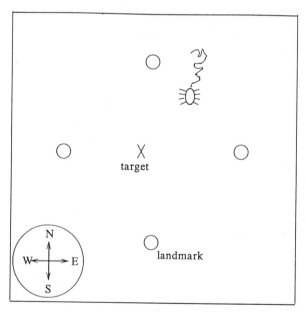

Figure 1.3 *Barto and Sutton's (1981) 'organism' learns to move toward the centre target location, guided by input describing distance to each of four landmark locations.*

active, the organism can move in a combination direction: north-east.) Each move is of a fixed distance in the appropriate direction.

After each move is made, the network receives reinforcement. This consists of the change in strength of the odour emitted by the target – which also falls off with distance. If the move leads the organism toward the target, the reinforcement is therefore positive; if away, the reinforcement is negative. Eventually, even placed in a novel starting position, the trained organism moves directly towards the target. This behaviour occurs even if the target odour is disabled, because the organism has learned to encode the target location in terms of the odours from the four landmarks.

The Barto and Sutton system is an example of an approach which is particularly relevant to the context of this book. The system does not require a distinct off-line training phase (as INFANT and MURPHY do), and what is learned depends upon the responses of the system: in contrast, MURPHY uses a pre-selected training set, while INFANT's training examples are selected at random. The Barto and Sutton system represents true exploratory learning, and approaches much closer to the normal conditions of animal learning.

However, these three example exploratory learning systems do not illustrate delay learning (nor did their designers intend them to). To embody delay learning, more complicated methods are needed. The next chapter turns attention to existing methods which begin to achieve the desired sophistication of delay learning, and many of which employ exploratory reinforcement learning to achieve that goal.

2

Neural networks and learning with delayed reinforcement

Much neural network research is based on weight-adjusting nodes (Figure 2.1). In a common instantiation, each node j receives inputs along each of several input pathways x_{ji}. These inputs may come from an external input pattern or may in turn be derived from the output of other nodes. Associated with each input x_{ji} is a weight w_{ji}. The activation of the node is then defined as $a_j = \sum_i x_{ji} w_{ji}$; and the node output is $y_j = f(a_j)$, where f might be a threshold function or a sigmoid. This output may provide part of the network's externally visible output or may be passed as input to other nodes.

Networks of these nodes are usually trained by presenting external input patterns, and adjusting the weights until the network produces acceptable external output in response. There are numerous methods for performing this training. Probably the most widely used are error backpropagation and its variations. Error backpropagation was formalized independently by Rumelhart, Hinton and Williams (1986) and several others (e.g., Werbos (1974), Parker (1985), LeCun (1986)). It requires that the net be arranged in feedforward layers – that is, that any node in one layer can send output to nodes in higher layers only – and that f be a non-decreasing differentiable function, such as a sigmoid.

Then, if j is a top-layer node, and therefore its output is externally visible, its desired response d_{pj} to a given external input pattern p can be used to update its weights.

$$\Delta w_{ji} = \eta(d_{pj} - y_{pj}) f'\left(\sum_i w_{ji} x_{ji}\right) x_{ji} \qquad (2.1)$$

The weight change on the ith pathway to j is adjusted proportional to the difference between desired and actual output from j, to the derivative of the total node activity, and to the strength of input x_{ji}.

If j does not produce externally visible output, d_{pj} is not available (j is in this case said to be a hidden node), and the backpropagation algorithm replaces

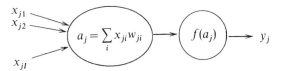

Figure 2.1 *A weight-adjusting node.*

the $(d_{pj} - y_{pj})$ term with an estimate of the contribution of j to the error at higher levels.

$$\Delta_{ji} = \eta \delta_{pj} x_{ji} \quad \text{where} \quad \delta_{pj} = f'\left(\sum_i w_{ji} x_{ji}\right) \sum_k \delta_{pk} w_{kj} \tag{2.2}$$

Error backpropagation is a good example of a **supervised learning** paradigm. Training requires a set of exemplar input or training patterns each paired with a desired output pattern. The output pattern specifies a desired response for each visible output, although the network is allowed to find unspecified outputs for the hidden units. Typically, the network is shown the complete training set repeatedly until suitably correct outputs are achieved from every visible node to every training pattern.

For this reason, supervised learning is a good choice if the problem domain is such that a rich training set is readily available, and extended training time is not a problem. If the training set and the network have been well designed, the network can be expected to generalize its knowledge to novel input patterns, which were not part of the training set, and produce visible outputs which resemble the outputs learned to training inputs which are in some sense similar to the novel input.

It should be obvious that this is a very restricted from of learning. The short-coming of supervised learning which is of interest here is that the human trainer (or some other form of teacher) must provide the optimal output to every input. This in effect means that in order to train the network to solve a problem, the problem must already have been solved by the teacher (although the goal may be to obtain a neural network which can generalize in a way that the teacher cannot). Supervised learning is also quite different from the form of learning which takes place in animals, and in humans – except for rote learning which is relatively difficult for humans. An animal may learn by exploration, by trial and error, and even by watching others of its species. It does not learn by being exposed to situations and then comparing its responses with those of a teacher providing a correct optimal response – not least because this would involve providing a desired output to each of the animal's motor neurons, which provide its only visible output.

At the opposite end of the spectrum from supervised learning is **unsupervised learning**. Here, the training output pattern is completely eliminated. The goal for the network, instead of learning to reproduce desired outputs, is to self-organize so as to classify like inputs by producing like outputs –but there is no teacher to specify what those like outputs must be. Outside of the neural network domain, this function might be accomplished by principal component analysis or Baysian classification.

A standard unsupervised learning algorithm is learning vector quantization (Kohonen, 1984); others have been described (e.g., Grossberg (1987), Rumelhart and Zipser (1986)). Kohonen's algorithms have however actually been used in real-world applications such as speech recognition (Kohonen, 1988) and decoding of handwritten cursive script (Morasso, 1989).

In this algorithm, each node j receives input from all I external inputs, each is provided with a vector $\mathbf{v}_j = (v_{j1} \ldots v_{jI})$, and the v_{ji} are initialized randomly. As each I-component input vector p is presented to the network, all nodes compute the inner product $r_j = \mathbf{p}.\mathbf{v}_j$. The node j for which r_j is maximal becomes the 'winner'. The remaining nodes are then updated. Usually, the network is conceived of as being organized in 1-, 2- or 3-dimensional space, so that the 'distance' between two nodes can be computed, and a region can be defined around the winning node which includes nodes no more than a certain distance away. All nodes k within this region are updated to make them respond more like the winning node j.

$$\Delta \mathbf{v}_k = \eta_t^+ (\mathbf{p} - \mathbf{v}_k) \qquad (2.3)$$

All nodes k byeond this distance are updated to make them respond less like j.

$$\mathbf{v}_k = -\eta_t^- (\mathbf{p} - \mathbf{v}_k) \qquad (2.4)$$

The η_t^+ and η_t^- are parameters which decrease as training time t increases. η_0^+ might start at 0.1, and decrease to 0 by η_{5000}^-.

After several thousand presentations of each input, the network should have generated responses to input patterns which are 'topology-preserving'. This means that inputs which are similar will generate responses from nodes which are close in distance. For instance, in a speech recognition task learned by a two-dimensional grid of nodes, fricatives might come to elicit responses from the upper right-hand corner of the grid, while the phoneme 'a' might generate responses from a cluster of nodes somewhere else.

The value of unsupervised networks is that they do not require any provision of desired outputs from a teacher, and therefore it is unnecessary to work out what the desired outputs should be: in fact, the structure of the trained network might even provide insights as to how the inputs naturally cluster. There is also a strong argument that regions of the brain are organized in similar fashion: for example, there seems to be this type of learning within primary visual cortex, which learns to allocate groups of cells to respond to whatever visual features are present in the environment during development (Blakemore, 1975).

However, true though this argument may be, it is fundamentally limited. Animals do learn to respond to sensory inputs in a way that is critically shaped by their environment, not merely the random initialization of their neural networks. Specifically, animals tend to generate responses to their inputs and receive reinforcement. Reinforcement was defined in Chapter 1 as a stimulus which can result in a change in the behaviour of an animal or a learning system. This might take the form of positive reinforcement, such as satiation, warmth, or a smile from one's mother, or of negative reinforcement, such as hunger, cold, or disapproval from one's mother. This is not the same as provision of a desired optimal input, but it is still environmental information that is used to update the system's responses.

A third form of neural network learning, intermediate between supervised and unsupervised learning, is **reinforcement** learning. As its name suggests, there is no teacher but rather a 'world' or a 'critic' which provides (usually scalar) evaluation of the appropriateness of the system's outputs. In a biological sense, the critic's response consists of positive and negative reinforcement signals. In an engineering sense, the critic might send a $+1$ signal to a system when its actions achieve the desired results and -1 when it deviates.

In the simplest type of reinforcement learning, each node j computes its activation and output in the same way as a node in a supervised learning paradigm; it is only the learning rule which changes. The reinforcement signal r may be > 0 for positive reinforcement, < 0 for negative reinforcement, and 0 in absence of reinforcement. Then each weight changes as

$$\Delta w_{ji} = \eta x_{ji} y_j r \qquad (2.5)$$

The learning rule is applied to every node, regardless of whether it produces visible output, and regardless of whether its individual output y_j may have been right or wrong. This means that nodes may often receive reinforcement signals which, although descriptive of the appropriateness of the external output as a whole, may not reflect whether they themselves output correctly. Because nodes are liable to receive reinforcement which is misleading in this

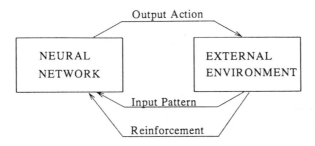

Figure 2.2 *The relationship between a reinforcement-learning neural network and a world including a critic.*

way, reinforcement learning paradigms are often very much slower than supervised learning, which provides the network with richer feedback describing its performance.

However, because some feedback is provided, reinforcement learning systems can learn tasks which are impossible for unsupervised learning systems: namely, where it does not suffice to simply classify the input, but specific kinds of responses are required. Some examples are game-playing, where an optimal move may not be definable, but the goodness of a move can be judged, or control of a machine, where the effect of a network output is measured but this is the only information available to judge the network response.

Reinforcement learning is also the most like **operant conditioning**, a basic form of learning in animals. In operant conditioning, the animal receives reinforcement contingent on some response, and learns to repeat (or avoid) that response. For example, a pigeon may receive a pellet of food whenever it pecks at a circle in the experimental cage, or a rat may be given an electric shock whenever it enters a certain region of its cage. In these situations, the animal tries out responses to environmental situations, and is given an evaluation of its responses in the form of reinforcement (food, pain)–but it is not shown what the optimal response would be. Humans also learn by operant conditioning: if a child's mother comes running every time a child starts crying, the child quickly learns that crying is an effective way to obtain the positive re-inforcement of attention or of being held; a man may develop a strong aversion to bananas if he once develops violent nausea after eating a banana – even if he knows full well that those pains were due to a winter flu.

The learning systems of interest in this book must accomplish something quite like operant conditioning: because they are exploratory, they try out actions, as represented by system responses, and adapt their behaviour according to the reinforcement provided by the environment. For this reason, it is reinforcement learning which is most often used as the vehicle for this kind of task, and which is of principal interest in this book.

However, the reinforcement algorithm outlined above does not make any provision for situations where the reinforcement may be delayed, another important criterion for the system desired. In operant conditioning, there is always a slight delay inherent between the action and the receipt of reinforce-ment; but there is often also an explicit delay, as in the case of the man who develops nausea several hours after his meal. So, the simplest reinforcement learning algorithms are not powerful enough to accomplish delay learning.

There have been several methods which make a start on extending learning paradigms to accomplish delay learning, most of which are based on reinforcement learning techniques. These fall into three categories: those which map delay learning tasks onto standard pattern association tasks, those which maintain histories, and those which use prediction-driven reinforcement. Each addresses some aspects of the problem, but as will be seen, none is sufficiently general to fully solve the problem of delay learning as defined here.

2.1 Mapping onto pattern association tasks

Neural networks are inherently pattern associators: given a certain pattern of external inputs, they produce a pattern of external outputs. The process by which these outputs are produced may vary widely between networks, but the unifying feature is that of associating input and output patterns.

Therefore, perhaps the simplest manner in which to use neural networks to solve a problem involving delayed reinforcement is to translate that problem into a straightforward pattern association task. The delay is eliminated, and for every input the system simply memorizes the correct output. It does not need to be aware, under this approach, of the timing according to which reinforcement may be arriving.

An example of such a system is the simulated car driver designed by Shepanski and Macy (1988). In simulation, a car drives around a racetrack, and the neural network learning to control it must learn first to keep a safe distance from the cars ahead of it and second when and how to change lanes and pass other cars. This is a delayed learning task in the sense that reinforcement (crashing, or the avoidance of a crash) only comes a short while after decisions about acceleration are made. Further, learning to change lanes and pass cars is a reinforcement learning task in the sense that there is no *a priori* right action under given conditions: there may be several possible actions all of which would serve to avert a crash.

Shepanski and Macy train their system in two phases. It initially employs exploratory learning to learn how to follow a pace car which varies its speed at random. The system outputs a decision to maintain, increment or decrement the speed of its car. The neural network is then trained by error back-propagation to output the decision which would have resulted in optimal following distance to the car ahead. They report that after some 1000 training steps, the system maintains optimal distance to the pace car and can adjust its speed to reflect changes in the pace car's velocity.

Once the system is proficient at this task, it is trained to execute lane changes. This again is done through supervised learning, but no longer in an exploratory fashion. Instead, a human controls the car and executes lane changes, passing other cars as he judges appropriate. The network is then trained, by backpropagation, using the human's responses as the correct optimal output. It is predictable but still amusing that the network will learn to take on the traits exhibited by the human used to train it: becoming an aggressive or cautious driver depending on the characteristics exhibited by the human it learns to mimic.

The car driving system is sheltered from the fact that the results of its output arrive with some delay. For example, a burst of acceleration may send the controlled car into the pace car with an inexorability unaffected by subsequent attempts to brake. But the system is trained in a purely supervised fashion, and corrections are calculated to each response immediately after it is made. In this way, the problem is reduced from one involving delayed reinforcement to one of pure pattern association: memorizing a (constructed) desired output to each input.

A similar approach is used in the backgammon player built by Tesauro and Sejnowski (1988). In a game environment, reliable reinforcement usually only arrives at the end of a game (win, lose or draw). There may be secondary reinforcement during the game, such as the capture of an opponent's piece or the loss of board territory, but this may reward small-scale activity which does not accurately reflect the overall progress of the game.

The backgammon player is trained by error backpropagation, and therefore requires provision of desired responses to every input pattern to be provided after each move. Tesauro and Sejnowski built up a database of game positions paired with the best possible move for each. The neural network is trained using this database until it can mimic the best move suggested for each position. Then, used in a real game, it generalizes from these carefully chosen examples to select moves appropriate to the actual game positions encountered during play. At least one network which they trained in this way managed to beat a commercial backgammon player about 60% of the time, while against a human expert it won 35–40% of the time.

Whereas the car driver learning lane changes has a training set generated by mimicking human outputs to the same input data, the backgammon player is trained on an extensive database of examples, compiled with great care by a backgammon expert. By restricting the training set to predefined examples, the problem of delayed reinforcement is sidestepped: the expert designing the examples assigns an arbitrary but reasonable 'best output' for each exemplar input. The expert is using his own knowledge of what results will eventually follow from certain game moves, and thereby eliminating the need for this kind of knowledge on the part of the neural network. The network only learns what the expert decides are good and bad moves, without any idea of why that judgement was made.

The approach of reducing problems involving delayed reinforcement to simple pattern association tasks allows the use of standard backpropagation, and decreases the training time needed, as information is reliable and prompt. However, it requires a great deal of effort on the part of a human teacher, either to demonstrate proficiency explicitly, or to construct a training set which is suitably broad to illustrate all aspects of the task, or to design heuristics which judge each output without recourse to (delayed) external reinforcement. Because so much information is provided by the teacher, this approach is not really addressing the problem of delayed reinforcement – although it may provide usable solutions to individual tasks such as backgammon and driving. It is the teacher who has mastered the ability to predict non-immediate consequences following from actions, rather than the network.

2.2 History maintenance

A more sophisticated neural network can deal with delayed reinforcement simply by keeping a record of each input it has received together with the output it produced; when reinforcement arrives at some future time, it can then use this to adjust each of its recent moves: rewarding them if the reinforcement is positive, and punishing them if it is negative. There are two ways in which this can be done. The more straightforward is to keep an explicit buffer containing the last n inputs and outputs; alternatively, each node can maintain an eligibility trace of its input pathways.

One system which keeps an explicit buffer is the blackjack player designed by Widrow *et al.* (1973). In a simplified version of blackjack, the dealer draws one playing card, and the player then draws a series of cards, deciding after each whether to stop drawing. If the sum of these cards exceeds 21, the player loses. Next, if the player has not yet lost, the dealer draws, following a fixed strategy, and likewise losing if the sum exceeds 21. Otherwise, the one whose sum is closest to 21 wins. A strategy is known which should result in 49.5% wins for the player. The situation is complicated by the strong element of chance in blackjack: even if the player makes all the correct decisions, the dealer may still win, while the player may win even though using a bad strategy.

Widrow and his co-workers trained a single node to play this game. It was provided with input representing the visible dealer's card and the current sum of the player's card, and output a binary decision to continue or stop drawing cards. Typically there would be several cards drawn before the stop decision, and therefore the ultimate results (win or loss) were delayed for several time steps.

The system therefore buffers each input pattern and the decision taken until the end of play. Then each input–output pair is sequentially reapplied to the node, and the weights on each input line are updated according to a rule like Equation (2.5), with $r = +1$ if the game is won and $r = -1$ if it is lost. It was deemed necessary to set the constant of proportionality η greater when $r = +1$ than when $r = -1$ as training progressed and most decisions taken by the system were optimal. Then after about 10,000 training games, the system tends to win 40–50% of the time.

Buffering is also used by the simulated food-finding 'bug' constructed by Cecconi and Parisi (1989). This bug exists in a two-dimensional grid world, moving from location to location in search of randomly placed 'food' objects. Its inputs consist of the direction to and angle with the nearest food object, and it can output a decision to move one location forward, turn left or right, or do nothing. If it enters a location containing food, it receives positive reinforcement.

At any time t, the bug system buffers the last eight decisions it made. When it encounters food, the system 'picks up' the bug and returns it to its location at time $t-8$. The network is then trained by backpropagation, where the desired output is the previous action at that location. In this way, the system learns that if it encounters similar input again, it should repeat the actions which resulted in encountering food. The system has been shown quite successful in learning to maximize the amount of food found.

Yet another example of this approach is Nguyen and Widrow's truck-backer-upper (1989). The task for this system is to control a simulated cab-trailer rig which must back up until the rear of the trailer is aligned with the loading dock. The system is first taught the kinematics of cab-trailer interaction by error backpropagation: given the location and angle of the cab and the trailer with respect to the loading dock and a steering signal (left or right), it learns to predict the resulting new locations and angles. Next, the system learns by trial and error how to back the rig into the desired location opposite the loading dock. At each time t, the system outputs a steering decision of left or right. The truck backs a fixed distance after each decision until it hits the loading dock wall. At this point, time T, an error signal is generated based on how far the rear of the trailer is from the dock. This, together with the last input pattern and steering decision is used to compute weight changes to the network using backpropagation. Since the steering decision at time $T-1$ was part of the input at time T, its error can also be computed. This is then used to train the network on the previous input pattern, $T-1$. The process continues backwards in time until the start of the sequence is reached. The actual change to each weight in the network is the sum of all the changes computed for each step in the sequence.

After thousands of learning sequences, Nguyen and Widrow report that the truck can learn to back smoothly to the loading dock, whatever its start position – even if the cab and trailer are jack-knifed or facing the loading dock head on.

The use of buffers to maintain intermediate states until results arrive is a much more convincing manner of addressing learning with delayed reinforcement than, for instance, the problem reduction described in the previous section. It has proved popular because it is relatively simple and is successful in limited domains (such as game-playing or restricted movement within a two-dimensional environment). Its chief short-coming is that it requires a buffer of finite size. If the buffer can contain n recent input–output pairs, the system will immediately not be able to solve problems where the reinforcement is delayed by $n+1$ or more time steps. However, if n grows very large, the storage required to maintain the buffer also grows.

Another difficulty with this approach is that as n grows, so does the number of recent actions reinforced each time a result arrives. This occurs in spite of the fact that it is a reasonable assumption that only the more recent events are likely to be responsible in any large degree for a result. More temporally distant events should usually not be reinforced, and the system may even be disrupted by adjusting them.

Keeping eligibility traces allows circumvention of these difficulties while maintaining the spirit of keeping a history of recent events. Within each node in the network, each input pathway (and possible each output) is provided with a trace value or eligibility: each time the input (output) is active, the eligibility is incremented; it decays to zero in the continued absence of activity. Then, whenever reinforcement arrives, each weight is adjusted in proportion to the eligibility for the input pathway with which it is associated: and weights on inputs which were most recently active will therefore be affected most strongly.

These eligibilities do not constitute a buffer, because if the same input is active twice in a row, the eligibility will reflect only the more recent activation – the older value is overwritten. Space requirements in the system are constant (and linear in the number of eligibilities maintained); the longest possible activity trace depends not on the space used but on how long it takes for an eligibility to decay to zero.

Examples of this approach are found in some neural networks which model **classical conditioning**. In classical conditioning, an unconditioned stimulus (UCS) to the system will innately produce a response (R); for example, a dog will salivate (R) at the sight of food, the UCS. During training, a conditioned stimulus (CS) is repeatedly presented just before the UCS. Eventually, the CS alone will evoke R: it becomes a predictor of the UCS. If the dog repeatedly hears a tone (CS) just before food is placed in front of it, it will begin to salivate at the tone even if there is no food in sight. Obviously, if the CS is then repeatedly presented without the UCS, the effect fades, as the CS ceases to be a predictor of the UCS. The border distinguishing classical conditioning from operant conditioning is often fuzzy, but an important aspect is that classical conditioning requires a pre-existing UCS–R relationship, while operant conditioning requires that the subject makes an overt action before any reinforcement arrives.

Classical conditioning can however involve delay learning when the CS precedes the UCS by some time interval: the subject must then maintain some memory of the CS during the interval.

This phenomenon is modelled by Barto and Sutton (e.g. 1981) using equations such as the following:

$$y_j(t) = f\left(\sum_{i=1}^{I} w_{ji} x_{ji} \right) \tag{2.6}$$

$$\bar{x}_{ji}(t) = \alpha \bar{x}_{ji}(t-1) + x_{ji}(t-1) \tag{2.7}$$

$$\bar{y}_j(t) = \beta \bar{y}_j(t-1) + (1-\beta) y_j(t-1) \tag{2.8}$$

$$\Delta w_{ji}(t) = c[y_j(t-1) - \bar{y}_j(t-1)] \bar{x}_{ji}(t-1) \tag{2.9}$$

Equation (2.6) is the node output rule, given inputs x_{ji} and weights w_{ji}. Equation (2.7) describes the eligibility trace $\bar{x}_{ji}(t)$: when input x_{ji} is active, the eligibility is set to its maximum; otherwise it decays by an amount $0 < \alpha < 1$. According to Equation (2.8), there is also an output trace, which is a function both of its decaying previous value ($0 < \beta < 1$) and of the previous node output. Finally, Equation (2.9) describes the weight update rule. Each weight is adjusted according to the eligibility of its input pathway ($\bar{x}_{ji}(t - 1)$) and the *change* in node output, represented by the difference between current output and the recent activity described by $\bar{y}_j(t - 1)$.

This model can perform classical conditioning given the convention that input x_{j0} is defined as the UCS, and has a fixed efficacy w_{j0} which is sufficient to produce the R: $y_j = 1$. The development of the conditioned response R to a conditioned stimulus CS is equivalent to production of y_j when some other x_{ji} is present ($i \neq 0$). An example of such learning is shown in Figure 2.3. On the left is the initial state of the system; CS x_{j1} precedes UCS x_{j0}. Eligibility $\bar{x}_{j1}$ increases during the activity of x_{j1}, but the stimulus is not sufficient to elicit response y_j. When stimulus x_{j0} is activated, the node does fire ($y_j = 1$). When this happens, both $\bar{x}_{j1}$ and $y_j(t) - \bar{y}_j(t)$ are non-zero, and so by Equation (2.9), the weight w_{j1} is incremented. When x_{j0} is inactivated, $y_j(t) - \bar{y}_j(t)$ is again non-zero – this time it is negative. However, by this time eligibility $\bar{x}_{j1}$ has decayed to zero, and the weight is not decremented. Eventually, after several similar pairings of CS and UCS, the responses are as shown in the right of Figure 2.3, and presentation of x_{j1} itself does elicit a response y_j,

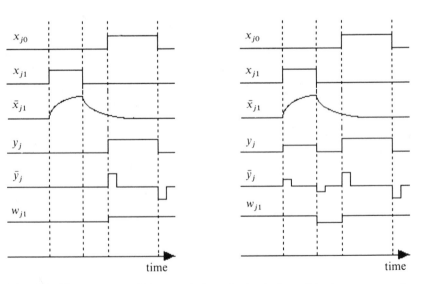

Figure 2.3 *The responses of Barto and Sutton's classical conditioning system at first (left) and post-training (right) pairings of CS and UCS, after Barto and Sutton (1982).*

although this response may never be fully as strong as the response elicited by the UCS x_{j0}.

Using this model, Barto and Sutton (1982) can also generate several additional phenomena associated with classical conditioning: selective learning of the CSs which are earliest or most reliable predictors of the UCS and failure to learn to respond to other superfluous ones, and learning of high-order associations (CS_1 predicts the UCS, and CS_2 predicts CS_1, and so on).

Klopf (1986) has proposed a model which is a bridge between the above approach and the use of buffers: his systems save the last few input–output pairs explicitly and assign a decaying eligibility to each. The learning rule is given as

$$\Delta w_{ji}(t) = \sum_{z=T_{min}}^{T_{max}} \alpha_z |w_{ji}(t-z)| [x_{ji}(t-z) - x_{ji}(t-z-1)][y_j(t) - y_j(t-1)]$$

(2.10)

The weight change at time t is the sum of changes relating each of a series of previous inputs (at time $t-z$) to the current change in output y_j. The constants α_z are learning rate constants, proportional to the efficacy of conditioning when the interval between CS (at $t-z$) and UCS (at t) is z, decreasing as z increases. The weight change is proportional to three other factors: the current weight value, the change in input x_{ji} at time z, and the change in output at the current time t.

The result is that weights will be strengthened if a change in the associated input pathway precedes a change in node output, much the same as in the Barto–Sutton model. Klopf (1988) claims that the learning curve produced by Equation (2.10) models biological learning data even more closely: the learning curve is first positively and later negatively accelerated, while in the Barto–Sutton model it is negatively accelerated throughout.

The major difference between the two models is that Equation (2.10) entails the keeping of a series of previous inputs in the $x_{ji}(t-z)$, each with eligibility α_z, whereas the Barto–Sutton model keeps only an average eligibility $\bar{x}_i(t)$. This extra information allows Klopf's model to consider delay conditioning tasks with timing eccentricities such as the CS becoming inactive before the UCS becomes active, and to mimic the biological response pattern – where the Barto–Sutton model would fail. By achieving this, Klopf's model manages true delay learning with constant space requirements; by contrast, the Barto–Sutton model was extended to involve prediction-driven reinforcement to accomplish these more complicated effects.

2.3 Prediction-driven reinforcement

Systems using eligibility traces and history buffers, such as those described in the last section, work well in domains where the reinforcement is frequent (so that the buffers are small or so that eligibilities will not decay to zero meantimes), and where there is a balance between positive and negative reinforcement.

Unfortunately, many interesting problems are not that simple. A classic example of such a problem is the pole-balancing or inverted pendulum problem. In its usual form, the task involves a pole connected by a hinge to a cart which can move to the left or right along a finite track. The learning system attempts to balance the pole upright by making small left and right movements of the cart; a failure signal provides negative reinforcement when either the pole falls over or when the cart moves off the end of the track.

There have been several partial solutions to this problem using the methods of previous sections: these include mapping onto a pattern association problem by computing the error after each move (Saerens and Soquet, 1989), by having a human teacher issue a positive or negative reinforcement signal after a sequence of moves which the teacher judges good or bad (Widrow and Smith, 1964), and storing the entire sequence of moves until a crash occurs, and then punishing each previous move proportional to recency (Mitchie and Chambers, 1968).

A more elegant solution is to reinforce the neural network on the basis of an internal feedback signal which is computed after every move, even if external reinforcement is not available. Such a feedback signal can be defined as the system's 'prediction' or 'expectation' of future reinforcement (hence the label 'prediction-driven reinforcement').

The technique dates back at least to Samuel's famous checkers player (Samuel, 1963). That system, although rule-based rather than using a neural network, executed a move and then evaluated the resulting board state

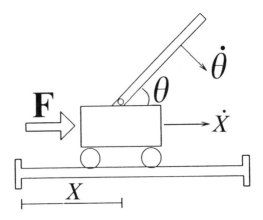

Figure 2.4 *The pole-balancing problem; inputs include cart location x, cart velocity $\dot{x}$, pole angle θ, and pole velocity $\dot{\theta}$; output moves the cart left or right with constant force* **F**.

according to a set of heuristics. Each evaluation was compared with the previous one, and the difference between the two was calculated. A sequence of moves would be rewarded if its immediate or near-immediate successors generated positive changes in evaluation, and punished if they did not. Samuel described the method as "attempting to make the score, calculated for the current board position, look like that calculated for the terminal board position of the chain of moves which most probably will occur during actual play."

The adaptive critic element (ACE) proposed by Barto and Sutton (e.g., Barto *et al.*, 1983) is a node which likewise *predicts* the reinforcement which will accrue from the actions of one or more conventional nodes with which it communicates. Such a system is shown in Figure 2.5.

The standard nodes (termed adaptive reward–penalty or A_{R-P} nodes) compute output $y_j(t)$ according to a function operating on the weighted sum of their inputs. The ACE monitors the reinforcement their outputs elicit, and outputs a signal indicating *predicted* future reinforcement, $p(t)$. The A_{R-P} elements then use this information, together with the external reinforcement $r(t)$ when available, to perform weight updates, using a rule such as (Barto *et al.*, 1981)

$$\Delta w_{ji} = c[r(t) + \alpha p(t) - p(t-1)][y_j(t-1) - y_j(t-2)]\bar{x}_{ji}(t-1) \quad (2.11)$$

where $c < 1.0$, $r(t)$ is defined as zero in the absence of external reinforcement, and $\bar{x}_{ji}$ is the same as in Equation (2.7). This rule means that weights are changed not when a change in r co-occurs with a change in y, but rather when a prediction p is proven wrong.

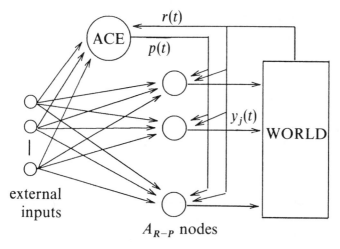

Figure 2.5 *A network containing prediction-generating ACE and a series* A_{R-P} *nodes interacting with the environment, after Barto et al. (1981).*

Learning in the ACE proceeds according to the rules

$$y_{ACE}(t) = f\left[\sum_{i=1}^{I} w_{ACE,i} x_{ACE,i}\right] \qquad (2.12)$$

$$\Delta w_{ACE,i} = \beta[r(t) + \gamma y_{ACE}(t) - y_{ACE}(t-1)]\bar{x}_{ACE,i}(t) \qquad (2.13)$$

Weights in the ACE are adjusted when the input pathways are eligible ($\bar{x}_{ACE,i}(t) > 0$) and when external reinforcement $r(t)$ appears or the prediction of reinforcement changes ($y_{ACE}(t) - y_{ACE}(t-1) \neq 0$).

This, admittedly quite complex, system can then be applied to a full version of the pole-balancing problem, where the only reinforcement occurs when the pole or cart go out of bounds. To solve the problem, Barto *et al.* (1983) used a single A_{R-P} node together with the ACE; both nodes contained enough input pathways so that each possible input state, describing the pole angle and velocity with respect to the ground and the cart location and velocity along the track, would activate a unique input (and hence a unique weight).

The ACE was a variation of that described above, while the A_{R-P} was defined by the rules

$$y_{A_{R-P}}(t) = f\left(\sum_{i=1}^{I} w_{A_{R-P}} x_i\right) \qquad (2.14)$$

$$\Delta w_{A_{R-Pi}} = \eta[r(t) + \alpha y_{ACE}(t) - y_{ACE}(t-1)]\bar{x}_i(t) \qquad (2.15)$$

The A_{R-P} weights are adjusted when predictions of the ACE are wrong, not when explicit reinforcement arrives. If $r(t) = -1$, but $y_{ACE}(t-1) = -1$ also, then the failure was fully predicted by the ACE, and no change occurs to the A_{R-P}. If the predictions change indicating that the current situation generates a stronger prediction of failure, then the last A_{R-P} output is punished; if the current situation generates a more positive prediction, then the last output is rewarded.

Barto, *et al.* (1983) report that after about 100 learning trials, the $ACE-A_{R-P}$ system manages to balance the pendulum upright for more than 500,000 time steps (equivalent to nearly three hours of simulated time).

The ideas of prediction-driven reinforcement belong to the paradigm of **learning by temporal differences** (Sutton, 1988). These methods are characterized by learning based not on the difference between predicted and actual outcomes, but on the changes in successive predictions themselves. A general form for the weight changes within this paradigm is given by Sutton (1988) as

$$\Delta w_{ji}(t) = \alpha(p(t+1) - p(t)) \sum_{k=1}^{t} \lambda^{t-k} \nabla_w p(w) \qquad (2.16)$$

If $t = 1$, this resembles the standard Barto–Sutton rules; for $t > 1$ it resembles the Klopf model which also requires maintenance of a series of recent events, but here they are recent predictions rather than recent events. Equation (2.16) makes no explicit reference to external reinforcement at all, but by assumption if $r(t) \neq 0$ then $p(t) = r(t)$.

Sutton (1988) notes that there are several types of situation which systems using temporal difference methods can handle, while systems not involving prediction could not. One example is a world where some state N is usually followed by (immediate) reinforcement with a probability of 90%. If a novel state A is entered and this then leads to N, and on this one occasion positive reinforcement follows, a non-predicting delay-learning system will (incorrectly) positively reinforce the move from A to N. A temporal difference system will (correctly) assign to A some proportion of the negative reinforcement expected from state N. On the other hand if this first-time transition from A to N results in negative reinforcement, the non-predicting system will assign 100% probability of negative reinforcement to A, while the temporal difference system will again associate some proportion of the 90% probability with A.

Sutton (1988) also lists some situations where temporal difference methods will fail. One of the most relevant involves a state N which, when entered from B elicits positive reinforcement, whereas entry of N from any other state leads to negative reinforcement. Using temporal difference methods, the states will be associated with the *overall average* expected reinforcement in state N: the system will be unable to predict that the expected reinforcement actually depends on a previous state. This is an extremely important point when considering the applicability of temporal difference methods to learning with delayed reinforcement. It means that, while suitable when each of a series of actions is equally responsible for a reinforcement, or when responsibility decreases in a linear way with recency, it fails when there are actions in the sequence which do *not* influence the final outcome. For instance, returning to the system which learns to control a car, a burst of acceleration may result in a crash even if the last few actions pre-impact are attempts to brake. It is important that the system not punish these last few (appropriate!) actions, but selectively punish the actions which actually caused the overall outcome.

2.4 Scope for new models

A huge research topic in machine learning studies has always been the **credit assignment** problem: learning which actions and which sequences of actions cause observable effects. The problem of delay learning, as defined here, is only a very small part of this problem. A system which accomplishes delay learning in effect has learned that certain actions are usually followed, at some temporal distance, by certain effects. This is not to say that the system has any understanding of which actions *cause* those effects – only which actions precede (or even predict) those effects. For this reason, delay learning is much more accurately compared with operant conditioning than with credit assignment.

As an example which illustrates this point, animals such as rats and quail can be operantly conditioned to avoid certain foods if ingestion is followed by nausea-producing irradiation (Walker, 1987) or to prefer certain other foods if ingestion is followed by vitamin injections which remedy a metabolic deficiency (Garcia *et al.*, 1967). Such 'superstitious' learning is a failure of credit assignment (the activity of eating is not what *causes* the nausea or attainment of vitamins). However, it is an illustration of delay learning: the animal has discovered the temporal relationship connecting its actions with later reinforcement: namely, whenever it eats the substance in question, at some later point (the experimenter sees to it that) feelings of sickness or health follow.

Each of the methods described for dealing with learning under conditions of delayed reinforcement has some strengths and some weaknesses. Mapping the task onto a pattern association problem simplifies matters, but as in the examples discussed, it requires provision of extensive information by the teacher and produces a system which is specialized to learn one task. Any knowledge about the solution cannot in general be expected to transfer to another task. Use of buffers to maintain recent input–output pairs is a general solution, but entails a trade-off in the size of the buffer: storage space versus maximum length of delay which can be bridged. Eligibility traces allow for systems to associate reinforcement with events which happened indefinitely long ago, since the upper bound on the delay bridgeable is the time until an eligibility trace decays to zero; this approach, however, requires that reinforcement information arrive at regular intervals and that it be appropriate to reinforce events proportional to their recency.

Temporal difference methods are probably the most sophisticated popular method for delay learning. Reinforcing on the basis of prediction rather than actual external reinforcement means that such systems can learn even when the world never provides positive reinforcement, or when reinforcement arrives very seldom. However, as Sutton's example shows, they are also tied to associate reinforcement with events dependent on presentation order.

Yet one of the interesting aspects of learning with delayed reinforcement is that events occurring during the interim between action and reinforcement may be irrelevant with respect to the arrival of that reinforcement. Curiously, the simpler buffer-maintaining systems can have some success at this. If state A leads to state N, and then positive reinforcement, a buffer-maintaining system can learn to associate positive reinforcement with A, regardless of complications such as N followed by negative reinforcement if entered from any other state.

What is needed really is a system which can learn the effects of an action, even if reinforcement is delayed, but which can also learn to separate out other actions which may occur close in time and yet may not affect this reinforcement. Ideally, such an approach, like temporal difference methods, could use predictions to guide its learning; like eligibility-computing systems, apply reinforcement to events arbitrarily far back in time; and like buffer-maintaining systems, have enough information available about past states to allow learning to be selectively applied to those actions which truly elicited the reinforcement.

3

RAM-based nodes
and networks

In a sense, this chapter is parenthetical with respect to the rest of the book. Chapter 4 begins to describe delay learning systems which are based on a type of neural network which represents a conceptual shift from the usual weighted-sum-and-threshold nodes used in most of the neural network research described earlier in this book. Because this network model, using RAM-based nodes, is only beginning to enter into widespread use, this chapter contains an introduction to the theory and history of the paradigm.

Understanding of the network model is a necessary step in understanding the performance of delay learning systems based on it. However, the basic idea underlying the systems is independent of the particular type of neural network used to implement them. RAM-based nodes were chosen for their convenience and learning speed, but in no sense is the capability of the machine dependent on this choice of substrate.

3.1 Introduction and motivation

Much research into artificial neural networks can be traced back to the famous McCulloch and Pitts (1943) paper specifying the function of neurons as logical propositions. The proposition, formally a 'disjunction of logical minterms', takes the form of a list of **antecedents** and a single **consequent**. The consequent will be true if at least one of the antecedents is true; each antecedent in turn consists of a series of components which must all be true if the antecedent is to be true. The neuron output corresponds to the consequent in this formalism, while each antecedent corresponds to one of the combinations of input activity which cause the neuron to fire. This involves the now-common simplification that neuron output is binary (firing or not firing), and inputs are also either active or inactive. A McCulloch and Pitts neuron fires when at least some minimum number of its inputs are active; there are also inhibitory inputs to the neuron, whose activity suffices to prevent the neuron firing. The primary result of the paper was to show that the behaviour of any network of these neurons could be described as a proposition, and that any such proposition could be computed by some network.

In some ways, this is a very powerful conclusion, as it shows that these processing units can be combined into general logic machines. However, this is not the same as showing, for example, Turing machine equivalence. Only those problems which can be re-formulated into logical propositions are guaranteed solution. The main importance of the paper was in making explicit the relationship between small processing units (of which biological neurons are perhaps the most highly evolved example) and the computationally describable behaviours to which they can collectively give rise.

Although the McCulloch–Pitts unit is the concept to which most artificial neural network (ANN) research traces its roots, there is actually no mention made in this paper of either weights on the input lines, or of any mechanism of learning (which would correspond to changing the proposition implemented by a neuron or node). Starting from this definition of a node, it is equally valid and perhaps even more natural to view the node as storing a list of the antecedents which suffice to make the node active. In this way, the node can be implemented as a look-up table, in which each possible combination of inputs is a possible antecedent, whose location in the look-up table stores information as to whether that input combination should cause node activity.

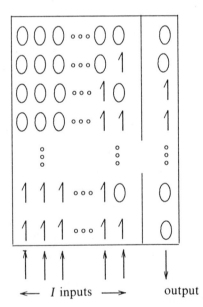

Figure 3.1 A *standard RAM-node: binary inputs form an address into look-up table memory. The stored value addressed by the current input becomes the node output.*

Such a node can be implemented as a standard random access memory (RAM), in which each combination of inputs forms an address into the memory of the RAM, and the value stored at that address indicates the node output for that pattern of inputs. This formalism defines the class **RAM-based nodes**. This type of node is trained by adjusting the information determining the node output for a particular combination of inputs. The node has learned to respond correctly when it has stored the correct value for each possible input pattern at the appropriate address.

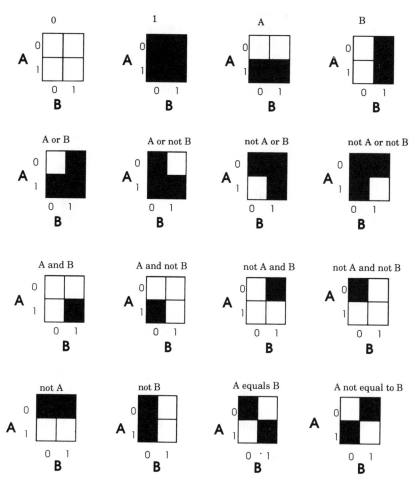

Figure 3.2 *The 16 possible boolean functions of two inputs. Each node shown implements one function, with the convention that input (A = 0, B = 0) addresses top left look-up table location, input (A = 0, B = 1) addresses top right location, inputs (A = 1, B = 0) and (A = 1, B = 1) address bottom left and right. Node then outputs value 1 (black) or 0 (white) stored at addressed location.*

The first important feature of this node is that it can learn to execute any of the 2^{2^I} binary functions of its I inputs, whereas a weighted-sum-and-threshold node is restricted to implement only linearly-separable functions of its inputs. For example, given two inputs A and B, there are 16 possible functions, as shown in Figure 3.2.

A weighted-sum-and-threshold node, for example, can learn any of the above functions except for the last two: A equals B, and A is not equal to B. The latter is also known as the exclusive-or problem: it is equivalent to stating that the node should output 1 whenever either A or B is 1, but not both. To solve this problem with weight-using nodes requires a network of at least two nodes. A RAM-based node, however, has no such restriction, since it simply implements a look-up table and can store the appropriate response for each combination of its inputs.

On the other hand, the RAM-based node has no inherent generalization. Storing the correct output to a particular input pattern has no effect on the node's response to other similar input patterns. Often, this is a desirable property; however, many of the interesting properties of weight-using nodes derive from their ability to map similar input patterns to similar outputs. Networks of RAM-based nodes do generalize, as will be explained below.

3.2 Bit-addressable RAM-based nodes

The RAM-based node traces its roots to the n-tuple sampling machines of Bledsoe and Browning (1959), where n-tuple is used to refer to the n-bit vector formed by the input pattern to a node. Bledsoe and Browning constructed machines consisting of banks of 2-input nodes connected to a 10×15 binary input image. Each node contained one location for each possible combination of its inputs: in this case, four such combinations existed. There was one bank of nodes for each possible class; their experiments were with alphanumeric character recognition, so there would be a bank of 'A' nodes, of 'B' nodes, and so on. All locations in all nodes were initialized to contain 0. During training of an 'A' pattern, each node in the 'A' bank would write a 1 into the location addressed by the bits in the input pattern to which it was connected. During training of a 'B' pattern, the same procedure was repeated but in the nodes of the 'B' bank. Later, given a pattern to classify, the 'A' nodes each output the address stored at the location addressed by the pattern; the sum of all responses from these nodes was summed to give the 'A' response. This could then be compared with the responses from the 'B' bank and others. If the 'A' bank's response was higher than that from all other banks, the pattern was classified as an 'A'.

The n-tuple sampling machines could generalize because information was distributed across the nodes of a bank. For example, given a pattern constructed from a trained 'A' pattern, distorted by a single bit of noise, all but one of the 'A' nodes would output 1; the summed response of the 'A' bank would therefore not degrade noticeably. As the input pattern differed more from the trained examples, the responses of each bank would be a function of the overlap between stored patterns and the current version.

This idea lay fairly dormant until Aleksander and Stonham (1979), treating n-tuples as addresses, noted that the RAM was a natural implementation for the n-tuple look-up table storing responses. The WISARD pattern recognition machine (Figure 3.3), prototyped in 1981, makes use of RAM-nodes in learning to classify images from a television camera (Aleksander *et al.*, 1984); in its commercial implementation, it can be trained on or used to recognize binarized images at a rate of 25 per second. It contains several discriminators, each trained to recognize one class of images. Each node in a discriminator

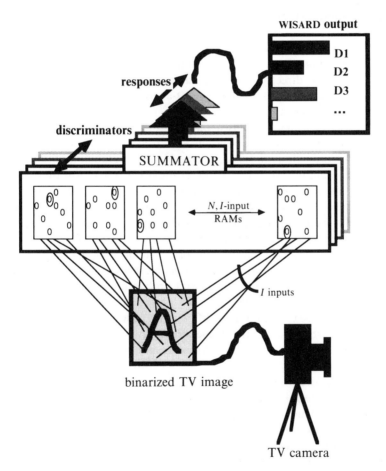

Figure 3.3 *Schematic diagram of the WISARD machine. Discriminators output responses proportional to the percentage of their nodes recognizing n-tuples in the current TV image.*

simply receives as input a few (typically 4–8) pixels, and stores a 1 at each location ever addressed by a training pattern. Then in classification of a novel image, the output of one discriminator is the percentage of nodes addressing 1s, giving the similarity of a test image to the set of images to which that discriminator has been trained.

The WISARD, because it does not need to be configured for a particular application, only trained, and because its operation is so fast, has been used in a variety of commercial applications. These have included domains such as sorting objects on conveyor belts, visually checking layouts of printed circuit boards, sorting mail by postcode, and checking that labels on phials match what is supposed to be inside. In these cases, the WISARD is connected to some effector such as a robot arm, which might sweep objects into one of two piles, depending on the classification that the object is okay or deviant from the norm.

The WISARD is possibly the best-known example of a machine based on RAM-node techniques. It is also based on the simplest kind of RAM-node: in which the nodes directly store the value to be output. Another way of categorizing these nodes is that they are **bit-addressable**: each address points to a location which stores only a single bit.

Another type of machine based on these bit-addressable nodes is one in which the node contents are random and fixed, so that each node is pre-determined to execute a random one of the 2^{2^I} possible functions of its I inputs. In this case, training is not a process of setting stored values – as these are held constant – but of optimizing over connections between the nodes. At the start, each node has a random I connections, to other nodes or to external inputs. At each training step, a connection is selected at random from one of the nodes, and is changed to some other random value. This is likely to have some effect on the network performance, in terms of the summed error $E = \sum_p E_p$ to all patterns p in the training set. If the change in error ΔE is negative, then the new connection becomes permanent with probability $e^{(\Delta E/T)}$. Otherwise, the connection reverts to its old value. This process ensures that error will eventually decrease to a minimum, although the process will be very slow. The parameter T, also known as the **temperature**, slowly decreases to zero during training. This is therefore the same process as simulated annealing in a weight-using net.

In one application, a network of this kind was applied to addition of two 8-bit integers (Carnevalli and Patarnello, 1987). Shown only 0.3% of the possible examples of addends mapping to correct sum, the network was able to memorize these examples and also generalize correctly to the remaining cases. The same workers also implemented a bug roaming a simulated world in search of food, and found that the system developed strategies which were consistent with the distribution of food during training (Patarnello and Carnevalli, 1990).

These examples, together with WISARD, are empirical proof that systems of nodes which, individually, have no generalization ability, can together result in generalizing behaviour.

Use of RAM-based nodes has several advantages over the weighted-sum-and-threshold approach. First, as the image recognition applications show, learning and classification operations can be very fast and even take place in real time. Second, the nodes are implementable in currently available RAM technology. Third, RAM-based nodes often lend themselves to analysis by virtue of their logic basis. Fourth, a RAM-based node is able to implement any of the 2^{2^I} functions of its I binary inputs.

3.3 The probabilistic logic node (PLN)

There are however limitations to bit-addressable RAM-based nodes. Taking the example of WISARD, training is write-once: once a pattern has been stored, it cannot be overwritten. It is possible to store a pattern which disrupts the system, and there is no solution except to re-initialize and re-train the system. This is a particularly evident problem in training with a video camera, where a single frame with the user's thumb in view is treated as a valid member of the class of image being trained.

A more subtle problem is the dual status of 0. If a storage location contains 1, then it is clear that at some point in training, a pattern contained the n-tuple which addresses that location. The value 1 is therefore a valid indicator of the presence of a pattern belonging to the class which the node is trained to recognize. However, 0 has no such clear interpretation. It may be that the n-tuple addressing a location which contains 0 is a counter-indicator of the class. It may just be that no information is known about the n-tuple.

To circumvent these problems, it is possible to consider a **word-addressable** node, where each location can store one of a *set* of values $\Omega = \{v_1, v_2, \ldots, v_\omega\}$. The RAM which implements the node therefore maps each address to a computer word, where the number of bits in the word depends on the number needed to represent the set of values. (If there are ω possible values, the RAM should address $\log_2 \omega$-bit words.)

The Probabilistic Logic Node (PLN) (Aleksander, 1988; Aleksander and Morton, 1990) uses stored values which may take on values from such a range. Next, the node is implemented to contain an output function Φ, which acts upon the stored value addressed by the current input, and converts it into binary output.

In the most basic PLN, the 3-state PLN, $\omega = 3$, and the values which may be stored are 0, 1, and u; the stored value is accessed as

$$add_j = \sum_{f=1}^{I} 2^{f-1} i_{fj} \tag{3.1}$$

where i_{fj} is the value of the fth input to node j; the node output is then

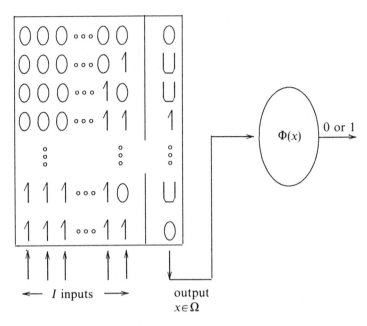

Figure 3.4 *A 3-state PLN. The stored value addressed by current node inputs passes through a probabilistic output function, producing binary node output.*

computed as

$$y_j = \Phi_j(loc_j[add_j]) = \Phi_j(v_j) \tag{3.2}$$

Here, loc_j is the look up table in the jth node, and at the add_jth address, it stores the needed value v_j. Φ_j is the output function for node j. In the 3-state PLN, it generates output as

$$\Phi(0) = 0$$
$$\Phi(1) = 1$$
$$\Phi(u) = 0 \text{ or } 1 \qquad \text{with equal probability} \tag{3.3}$$

This node was first described by Kan and Aleksander (1987).

Another way of describing the behaviour of a probabilistic node such as the PLN is in terms of its output probability function, Φ^P, where $\Phi^P(x)$ gives the probability that $\Phi(x)$ equals 1 for a given x. For a 3-state PLN

$$\Phi^P(0) = 0$$
$$\Phi^P(1) = 1$$
$$\Phi^P(u) = 0.5 \tag{3.4}$$

The stored values in a PLN are typically initialized to u. Thus, the existence of a u value in the PLN allows for the separation of 'no-information' from 'not-1'. If a location in a PLN stores a 0, it is because the n-tuple addressing it is evidence that the node should output 0.

Training of a 3-state PLN is a process of replacing us with 0s and 1s so that the correct output to each combination of inputs is obtained. The generic training algorithm for a PLN network is described by Aleksander (1988).

1. For all nodes j, for all addresses add_j, initialize $loc_j[add_j] = u$.

2. Choose an input pattern p to be trained.

3. Each node j forms an address add_j from the input, accesses a stored value $v_j = loc_j[add_j]$, and outputs $y_j = \Phi(loc_j[add_j]) = \Phi(v_j) = 0$ or 1, according to the rule in Equation (3.3).

4. When output values appear, judge the network response: if 'correct' then $r = +1$; if 'incorrect' then $r = -1$.

5. (a) If $r = +1$, do for each node j: if $v_j = u$, $loc_j[add_j] \leftarrow y_j$.
   (b) If $r = -1$, repeat from step 3, in the hope that some us may be transformed into different outputs, leading to a 'correct' overall response.
   (c) If after several loops, r still equals -1, do for each j: if $v_j \neq u$, $loc_j[add_j] \leftarrow u$.

6. Loop to step 2 until $r = +1$ for all patterns to be learned.

There are several points to be made about this algorithm. It is a reinforcement learning regime: the only feedback, r, is a global scalar applied to the network as a whole. It does however allow the network several attempts to maximize r (by repeating steps 3 and 4) before the reset operation of step 5(c). Because no such mechanism as backpropagation is needed, the updates are simple, local, and may be executed in parallel. Because learning is not done by gradient descent, and instead has a probabilistic component, local minima are escapable, and Shapiro (1989) has calculated that learning may be faster than gradient descent techniques such as error backpropagation on problems where the error surface is flat.

Aleksander (1989) has also defined a canonical form for PLN topologies: the pyramid. This consists of nodes which all have the same number of inputs I, and one output. At the lowest layer are enough nodes so that every bit of external input is connected to one node; these nodes then send output to the next layer and so on upwards until the topmost layer consists of a single node. A canonical network consists of enough pyramids to provide the desired number of output bits (one from each pyramid).

Given a canonical topology, and arbitrary I, it is possible to calculate the number of functions which the pyramid can implement (Al-Alawi and Stonham, 1990). Formally, a **function** is one of the ways of mapping each possible input to an output. For example, one function maps every possible input to the output 1; another function maps only those inputs containing an odd number of 0s to the output 1, and so on. The number of functions

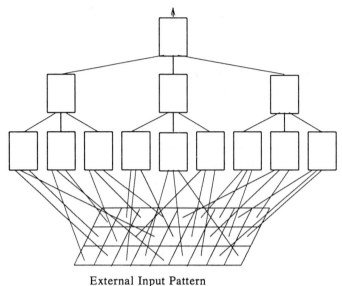

External Input Pattern

Figure 3.5 *A canonical pyramid of 3-input PLNs mapped randomly to a 27-bit external input pattern.*

implementable, for a pyramid of more than one level, shrinks dramatically compared with the total number of functions computable from a B-bit external input pattern. An easy example of this concerns a four-bit input pattern, and a topology of three two-input nodes arranged in a pyramid. The total number of functions of four bits is $2^{2^4} = 65,536$ functions. However, the pyramid contains three four-location RAMs, for twelve locations in total, and the number of ways in which these can be filled is only $2^{12} = 4096$. Even then, not all of those 4096 are distinct functions. For example, there are $2^{2 \times 4} = 256$ ways to fill the eight node locations in the bottom two nodes while the top node contains only 1s. All 256 of these map to the single function: for any input, output 1. In fact, out of the total 4096 ways to fill the 12 node locations with 0s and 1s, only 520 are distinct functions. Thus, this pyramid can implement only a fraction of the functions computable by a single 4-input RAM.

The implication of this reduction in number of computable functions by the pyramid topology is that the network cannot store a different output for each possible input, but must group some into the same response class. This is exactly the definition of generalization: that the network should respond to some novel input patterns in the same way as to trained patterns. (Of course it does not necessarily mean that the generalization will always take the form desired by the trainer.) PLNs generalize at the network level rather than at the level of individual nodes.

Aleksander (1988) showed that a 3-node pyramid of 2-input PLNs, trained with the generic algorithm, could learn to output the parity of a 4-bit input string within an average 32 learning cycles – 2 presentations of each of the 16 possible patterns. In contrast, a network trained by error backpropagation, and consisting of four hidden nodes and one output node can learn the same task after 2800 presentations of each input pattern – some 45,000 learning cycles in all (Rumelhart *et al.*, 1986). Myers and Aleksander (1988) showed that PLN networks compare favourably with backpropagation networks in terms of learning speed on a variety of small problems.

One reason for the fast learning of RAM-based nodes is the mutual independence of stored look-up table values. In a weight-using node, adjusting one weight affects the node's response not only to the current input pattern, but to all others in which the input bit connected to that weight is active. Changing a PLN stored value affects only those input patterns in which all I node inputs have the same values as in the current pattern. This will on average involve a much smaller number of patterns. A second reason for the gain in speed is the use of the u value to help ensure that changes have a minimum effect on stored knowledge. In the generic algorithm, as well as in the depth-first search algorithms, a first attempt is always made to produce the correct output by only changing the value of u locations. Any location not set to u has been so set because it was needed in order to obtain the correct output to some input pattern. Only if the correct output cannot be obtained after probabilistic or exhaustive search through the possible instantiations of the u values does the learning algorithm turn to erasing knowledge by resetting stored values to u.

The primary short-coming of the PLN as described is the lack of generalization at the node level. Nonetheless, it is often desirable to have the nodes themselves generalize. For example, if the input to a PLN is noisy, and one or two of the input bits are corrupted, the look-up table address will be completely altered, and the value stored there need have no correspondence to the output for the original pattern. A more elegant node would output the same value for the noisy as for the original input.

Aleksander (1990) has therefore proposed an extension of the PLN, the generalizing RAM or G-RAM, which is trained in the same way as the PLN. After training is completed, a **spreading phase** takes place. At this stage, each look-up table location is addressed sequentially. If the location contains a u, then a list is made of all locations addressed by inputs differing in one bit from the current address. If the list contains a mixture of 0s and us, then the current location is set to 0 as well. If it contains a mixture of 1s and us, the location is set to 1. If the list contains both 1s and 0s, however, the current location is equidistant from at least two trained patterns with opposite outputs, and remains set at u itself. After this spreading operation, and during operation, the node will respond to input patterns which differ in one bit from trained patterns in the same way as to the trained patterns, thus generalizing.

If the spreading algorithm is repeated several times, the amount of generalization increases. An I-input G-RAM which has undergone I spreading phases is termed 'fully-spread'. Lucy (1991) has shown that a fully-connected network of fully-spread G-RAMs functions as a perfect autoassociator. That is, the N-node network can store any combination of up to 2^N input patterns, and given any input pattern during operation, it will retrieve the stored pattern which is nearest in terms of number of stored bits.

It is also possible to train pyramids of 3-state PLNs by familiar search strategies (Al-Alawi and Stonham, 1990). In this approach, the output of the net to a training pattern is compared with the desired output. If it matches, then a store operation is done: all addressed locations which contain us set those us equal to the current node output, as in Aleksander's algorithm. If there is error, and the topmost node addresses a u, then it is set to output the opposite of its current output, as this eliminates the error, and then a store operation can be carried out. Otherwise, the previous layer is consulted. If any us are addressed there, the associated nodes output the opposite of their current output. If this eliminates the error on the top layer, then a store operation can be done with the current node outputs. Otherwise, the next previous layer is consulted, and so on backwards in an attempt to find a setting for the us which is consistent with the desired output. If the bottom layer of nodes is reached, and error persists, then the net is re-initialized, and training begins anew. This strategy is an attempt to avoid the massive error-correction within Aleksander's generic training algorithm: since every reset operation there erases information which was stored as necessary to generate correct output to some other pattern. Wang and Grondin (1989) have presented a similar search algorithm.

A different search strategy – the 'goal-seeking neuron' of Filho *et al.* (1990) – allows for the direct output of the u value, rather than its translation into random 0s and 1s. In their regime, a pattern is presented and each node forms its address and accesses a 0, 1 or u. This value is output directly, even if it is u. If a node receives a u as one of its inputs, it addresses both of the locations which would be accessed if the u were interpreted as a 0 or a 1. In general, if the input contains n us, then 2^n locations are addressed in the node. If the value stored in all addressed locations match, then that value becomes the node output; otherwise the node outputs u. When the topmost node is reached, if one of the addressed locations contains the desired output or a u, then that location is selected (and set to the desired output if necessary), and its address is propagated back to the previous layer. The nodes on this layer then select an addressed location consistent with outputting the value needed to form this address. Then in turn they pass their own addresses back to the previous layer of nodes, and so on backwards. During recall, the same multiple addressing strategy is formed, and each node outputs 0 or 1 if the majority of addressed locations contain that value, or u if no such majority exists.

3.4 ω-state PLNs and exploratory learning algorithms

Aleksander's generic PLN learning algorithm is a reinforcement learning algorithm. However, learning is not exploratory, since the minor loop allows the system several tries to maximize reinforcement. Additionally, negative reinforcement leads to a drastic erasure of learned knowledge: one stored value in each node is returned to the u state. Sometimes this may be unavoidable: the stored value may simply be incompatible with producing the correct responses to all inputs. However, this is seldom the case in all j nodes at once.

For example, 100 PLN pyramids, each consisting of three 2-input nodes, were trained to detect the parity of the 4-bit input string. For this problem, the networks have 2^{12} possible states, as mentioned above, of which exactly four comprise solutions to the problem. Therefore, during training, the closeness of the network to solution could be measured in terms of the number of look-up table locations across the three nodes differing in stored value from what is required in the nearest solution state. During training, each net was stopped on the first occasion when an error was generated such that $r = -1$. Twenty-two pyramids learned the problem without ever generating an error, and were removed from further analysis. The remaining 78 nets each contained three locations due for reset to u, for a total of 234. Of these, 53.4% actually already contained the same value as in the nearest solution, and so setting these bits to u was effectively moving the network *away* from the nearest solution. Only 20.1% were wrong, in the sense that their stored values differed in the nearest solution, and so reset was helpful. For the remaining 26.5% of locations, the network was equidistant from solutions involving both possible stored values 0 and 1, and so changing the value of that location did not affect distance to solution. Thus, in only about one-fifth of the cases was the reset actually warranted; in over one-half the cases it actually served to erase necessary information.

In a network operating under Aleksander's training algorithm, this is apparently not very harmful, and the networks still can learn quickly.

However, if the system is to undergo exploratory learning, such erasure of learned knowledge is crippling. No sooner will the system have begun to approach one solution than a minor error may divert it into a wildly different region of function space. Since exploratory learning requires the elimination of the loop whereby the network tries to maximize r, resets will become even more frequent, and the learning algorithm may well degrade into a random walk through possible functions.

Perhaps the obvious way to ease this situation is to make the reset operation less drastic. This is the goal behind the incremental training rule for the ω-state PLN (Myers and Aleksander, 1988).

The ω-state PLN allows look-up table locations to assume any of $\omega \geqslant 3$

values, $\{v_1, v_2, \ldots, v_{\omega-1}\}$, and computes output as

$$\Phi(v_i) = 1 \qquad \text{with probability } \Phi^P(v_i) \tag{3.5}$$

$$\Phi^P(v_i) = \frac{1}{1 + e^{1 - 2\alpha v_i}} \tag{3.6}$$

Equations (3.5) and (3.6) describe a node which will output 1 with a probability related to the value stored at the currently addressed location. Depending on the choice of α, the output probability function Φ^P may be linear, sigmoidal, or a threshold function. If it is a threshold function and if $\omega = 3$, the node is simply the 3-state PLN described in the previous section.

One result of extending $\omega \geqslant 3$ is that the node can output 1 with more finely gradated probabilities, which could be an important characteristic of an exploratory learning system.

A second result is that an incremental learning algorithm is now possible, by implementing incremental changes in the stored values. In this way, it is possible that no one reset erases much information, but that erroneous information is discarded only after a series of errors. Similarly, new information is only acquired after a series of experiences indicate its validity. Such a learning algorithm has been described by Myers and Aleksander (1988).

0. Consider $\Omega = \{v_i | v_{i-1} < v_i < v_{i+1}\}$

1. Initialize all stored values to v_u, where $\Phi^P(v_u) = 0.5$ or some other desired value.

2. Choose an input pattern p.

3. Each node j forms an address add_j, accesses a stored value $v_j = loc_j[add_j]$, and outputs $y_j = \Phi(loc_j[add_j]) = \Phi(v_j) = 0$ or 1, according to the rules in Equations (3.5) and (3.6).

4. When output values appear, judge the network response: if 'correct' then $r = +1$; if 'incorrect' then $r = -1$.

5. (a) Define $\Delta_j = \kappa_r$, where κ_r is the increment associated with reinforcement r.

   (b) For each node j:
   if $y_j = 1$, $loc_j[add_j] \leftarrow v_{(i+\Delta_j)}$;
   if $y_j = 0$, $loc_j[add_j] \leftarrow v_{(i-\Delta_j)}$.

6. Loop to step 2 until $r = +1$ for all patterns to be learned.

It will be noticed that step 5(b) allows $i + \Delta_j$ and $i - \Delta_j$ to grow beyond the range of $0 \cdots \omega - 1$; this can be resolved simply by clipping.

This training algorithm involves a linear change to the stored values and a sigmoidal output probability function such as Equation (3.5). Alternatively, if ω is large, it is possible to define a sigmoidal change to the stored values and a linear output function. In that case, step 5(b) of the training algorithm is replaced by

$$loc_j[add_j] \leftarrow v_{\hat{i}}, \qquad \text{where} \qquad \hat{i} = \frac{1}{1 + e^{\alpha(1 - 2(v_i + \kappa_r))}} \qquad (3.7)$$

Meanwhile, Equation (3.6) is replaced by the linear output probability function

$$\hat{\Phi}^P = (v_i) = v_{\hat{i}} \qquad (3.8)$$

These two cases are equivalent, since

$$\hat{\Phi}^P(v_i) = \Phi^P(v_{i + \Delta_j}) \qquad (3.9)$$

Therefore, any behaviour obtainable by a network of nodes using sigmoidal output function and linear stored value change is also obtainable by one with linear output function and sigmoidal stored value change, and vice versa. The former case (Equation (3.5) and step 5(b) of the learning algorithm) is usually simpler for discussion and implementation.

In the same way that 3-state PLNs were found to be faster than back-propagation networks on some small problems, the ω-state PLNs using the incremental learning algorithm were found to be faster still (Myers and Aleksander, 1988).

3.5 pRAMs, RAM-based nodes and continuous values

One limitation of the RAM-based nodes discussed so far is the restriction to binary input and output. A great deal of work has however been done with RAM-based nodes which are not so restricted. A well-developed example is the probabilistic RAM (pRAM) studied by Gorse and Taylor (1988; 1990), which allows for continuous inputs to the nodes.

A pRAM contains a look-up table of 2^I continuous values, each of which is the probability of outputting a 1 if that location is addressed. The input to a pRAM is a set of I binary inputs b_i. A simplified rule for the pRAM is (Gorse and Taylor, 1990):

$$P = \Pr(\text{node } j \text{ fires} | \text{inputs } b_1, \ldots, b_I) = \sum_x v_x \prod_{i=1}^{I} (b_i x_i + (1 - b_i)(1 - x_i))$$

$$(3.10)$$

Here, x is one of the set of possible addresses, v_x is the value stored there, and the rule computes a weighted average, so that the probability of outputting 1 is a function of the value stored at each address weighted by how likely that output was to have been addressed by the input. Because the inputs b and the addresses x are binary, for exactly one address will the product term be non-zero.

So, considering the 2-input pRAM shown in Figure 3.6, and the input

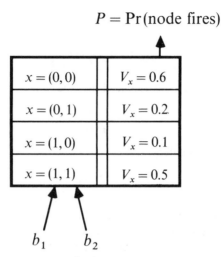

Figure 3.6 *A pRAM: binary inputs address continuous stored values representing probability of node firing.*

vector $(0.5, 0.75)$, the output becomes 1 with probability

$$P = 0.6(1 - 0.5)(1 - 0.75) + 0.2(1 - 0.5)0.75 + 0.1(0.5)(1 - 0.75)$$
$$+ 0.5(0.5)0.75 = 0.35 \tag{3.11}$$

Gorse and Taylor have investigated several training paradigms for pRAMs, especially reinforcement learning. For a pRAM, the reinforcement learning rule takes the form

$$\Delta v_x = \kappa[(P - v_x)r + \beta((1 - P) - v_x)p] \tag{3.12}$$

where v_x is the continuous value stored at the current address x, $r = 1$ for reward, and $p = 1$ for punishment. P is the overall probability that the node will output 1, as defined in Equation (3.10). Given the pRAM in Figure 3.6, with the input $b_1 = 0$ and $b_2 = 1$, $x = (0, 1)$ and so $v_x = 0.2$. Then, if node is to be rewarded for its last output

$$\Delta v_x = \kappa[(0.35 - 0.2) \times 1 + \beta(0.65 - 0.2) \times 0] = 0.15\kappa \tag{3.13}$$

An important aspect of this training rule is that it can itself be implemented as a pRAM which has inputs r, p, P and $V(x)$ and which outputs $\Delta V(x)$ (Clarkson, Gorse and Taylor, 1991).

Gorse and Taylor have also investigated supervised learning in pRAMs by gradient descent on the v_x, and unsupervised learning techniques. Clarkson *et al.* implemented a network of two pRAM nodes in SSI (Clarkson *et al.*, 1989) and of four pRAM nodes in VLSI (Clarkson *et al.*, 1991).

An even more sophisticated node is the i-pRAM, or integrating pRAM (Gorse and Taylor, 1990), which allows for continuous input and generalization within nodes. In an i-pRAM, the continuous input vector $\mathbf{C} = (c_1, \ldots, c_I)$,

$c_i \in \{0,1\}$ is approximated by the time average over R cycles of successive binary patterns $B = (b_1, \ldots, b_I)$, $b_i \in \{0,1\}$, where

$$c_i = \frac{1}{R} \sum_{r=1}^{R} b_i(r) \tag{3.14}$$

The output function is now updated to (Clarkson *et al.*, 1991)

$$\Pr(y_j = 1 | C) = \sum_x v_x \prod_{i=1}^{I} (c_i x_i + (1 - c_i)(1 - x_i)) \tag{3.15}$$

$$= \sum_x v_x \Pr(v_x \text{ addressed} | C)$$

Again, $C = (c_1, \ldots, c_I)$ is the continuous input vector, $x = (x_1, \ldots, x_I)$ is a pRAM address, and v_x is the continuous value stored at location x.

In an i-pRAM, the reinforcement learning rule now updates *every* location proportional to its responsibility for the current output (Clarkson *et al.*, 1991)

$$\text{for all addresses } x, \ \Delta v_x = \kappa [(P - v_x)r + b((1 - P) - v_x)P]$$

$$\times \prod_{i=1}^{I} (c_i x_i + (1 - c_i)(1 - x_i)) \tag{3.16}$$

In other variations on the theme of combining continuous values and RAM-nodes, Martland (1988) has implemented error backpropagation in RAM-nodes which store continuous values at each location. Given a continuous input, the node computes its output as

$$y_j = \sum_x v_x \Pr(x \text{ addressed by continuous inputs } (c_1, \ldots, c_I)) \tag{3.17}$$

In the case of a two-input node, for example

$$y_j = v_{00}^j (1 - c_0)(1 - c_1) + v_{01}^j (1 - c_0)c_1 + v_{10}^j c_0 (1 - c_1) + v_{11}^j c_0 c_1 \tag{3.18}$$

where v_{xy}^j is the value stored at location (x, y) in node j.

Then the error can be defined as $E = (t_j - a)^2$, where t_j is the node's desired output, if j is an output node.

Then the partial derivatives for the parameters of an output node A, to which nodes B and C input, are given as

$$\frac{\partial A}{\partial v_{00}^A} = (1 - y_B)(1 - y_C)$$

$$\frac{\partial A}{\partial v_{01}^A} = (1 - y_B)y_C$$

$$\frac{\partial A}{\partial v_{10}^A} = y_B(1 - y_C)$$

$$\frac{\partial A}{\partial v_{11}^A} = y_B y_C \tag{3.19}$$

while the partial derivatives for hidden nodes B and C which output to a higher level node A are

$$\frac{\partial A}{\partial v_{xy}^B} = [-v_{00}^A + v_{10}^A + (v_{00}^A - v_{01}^A - v_{10}^A + v_{11}^A)y_C] \frac{\partial B}{\partial v_{xy}^B} \tag{3.20}$$

$$\frac{\partial A}{\partial v_{xy}^C} = [-v_{00}^A + v_{10}^A + (v_{00}^A - v_{01}^A - v_{10}^A + v_{11}^A)y_B] \frac{\partial C}{\partial v_{xy}^C} \tag{3.21}$$

Finally, each parameter in the network is updated as

$$\Delta v_{xy}^z = 2\eta(t_A - y_A) \frac{\partial z}{\partial v_{xy}^z} \tag{3.22}$$

Martland found that training times on the exclusive-or problem with various numbers of external inputs were several times faster than weight-using networks on the same problem, but several times slower than RAM-node nets using Aleksander's algorithm (Martland, 1988).

Finally, an example of unsupervised learning in RAM-nodes with continuous stored values is Ntourntoufis's c-discriminator network (Ntourntoufis, 1990). He considers a single layer of I-input nodes, initialized to store a random continuous value at each of the 2^I locations. The nodes are grouped into discriminators, each of which comes to respond maximally to a class of pattern. The training algorithm is an extension of Kohonen's self-organizing, topology-preserving regime (Kohonen, 1984).

Given a training pattern, each RAM-node in each discriminator forms an address and outputs the (continuous) value found there. The discriminator outputs the sum of all its node outputs. The discriminator x with the highest response 'wins'. Each addressed location in each node j in x is incremented to increase future response of discriminator x to that pattern. Locations in j which differ in address by only a few bits from the current one may be progressively more weakly incremented. Locations with maximally different addresses may be decremented, to help fine-tune j's tendency to recognize patterns like the current one.

Discriminators which are defined as x's neighbours may undergo similar treatment; while discriminators which are not neighbours may undergo the reverse: to ensure they are less likely to respond to the same kinds of patterns as x does. After many training cycles, a topology-preserving low-dimensional representation of the input pattern space is constructed. Neighbouring discriminators respond maximally to similar input patterns, and different neighbourhoods of discriminators respond maximally to different classes of input patterns.

3.6 PLN parameters

Returning to the ω-state PLN, as used in the chapters which follow, there are three variables which define the node and its properties. These are I, the number of inputs to the node (and hence 2^I, the number of look-up table locations), ω, the number of possible stored values, and Φ^P, the output probability function.

3.6.1 I – the number of inputs to a node

In any PLN, I has a direct influence on the memory requirements ($2^I \log_2 \omega$ is a determinant of the size of the look-up table of the node), and also on the trade-off between generalization and memorization. In practice, the latter consideration usually dominates.

For a single-layer network of 3-state PLNs, for example, if one pattern P_1 has been trained, and the correct response $d_{P_1 j}$ has been learned at node j, then if a new pattern U is presented, the probability of eliciting $d_{P_1 j}$ is

$$\Pr(y_{P_1 j} = d_{P_1 j}) = (A_{P_1 U})^I + \tfrac{1}{2}(1 - (A_{P_1 U})^I) = \tfrac{1}{2} + \tfrac{1}{2}(A_{P_1 U})^I \qquad (3.23)$$

where A_{xy} is the proportion of pixels in common between patterns x and y – the Hamming overlap. Equation (3.23) is an immediate extension of the formula given in Aleksander and Wilson (1985) for deterministic RAM nodes, and it states that the probability that $y_{Uj} = y_{P_1 j}$ is equal to the probability that the n-tuple from U is sited entirely in the overlap between P_1 and U plus the probability that it is not, but the value addressed (u) is converted into $y_{P_1 j}$ anyway.

By extension of this (and by comparison with Aleksander and Wilson's rule), if patterns $P = \{P_1, \ldots, P_k\}$ are trained to produce output 1 at node j, and if patterns $Q = \{Q_1, \ldots, Q_l\}$ are trained to output 0, then the probability that node j produces a 1 in response to U is

$$\Pr(y_{Uj} = 1) = \sum_{i=1}^{k} (-1)^{i+1} PP(i)$$

$$+ \frac{1}{2}\left[1 - \sum_{i=1}^{k} (-1)^{i+1} PP(i)\right]\left[1 - \sum_{i=1}^{l} (-1)^{i+1} PQ(i)\right] \qquad (3.24)$$

where $PP(x)$ is the probability that the n-tuple is sited in any overlap between U and exactly x elements of P

$$PP(x) = \sum (A_{p1 p2 \ldots px U})^I \text{ for all } \{p1, p2, \ldots, px\} \subseteq \{P_1, P_2, \ldots, P_k\} \qquad (3.25)$$

Similarly for PQ

$$PQ(x) = \sum (A_{q1 q2 \ldots qx U})^I \text{ for all } \{q1, q2, \ldots, qx\} \subseteq \{Q_1, Q_2, \ldots, Q_k\} \qquad (3.26)$$

Defining generalization in terms of the likelihood of outputting to pattern U in the same way as to a similar trained pattern, it will be seen that for a given training set, the generalization of this (single-layer) net is wholly dependent on I. In particular, generalization decreases as I increases, while specificity (ability to memorize responses to larger or more similar training sets) increases with I. This is true for a 3-state PLN; for a ω-state PLN, the

$\frac{1}{2}$ term in Equation (3.24) becomes dependent on Φ^P, but the dependence on I remains. Similarly, as more levels are added to the network, the formulae become more complex, but the basic dependence on I remains.[1]

3.6.2 Φ^P – the output probability function

The output function, Φ, is a rule by which the node determines its output, given a certain pattern on its input lines. It is governed, for a non-deterministic node, by the output probability function Φ^P: $\Pr(\Phi(x) = 1) = \Phi^P(x)$. In the case of PLNs, it is the mechanism whereby stored values are interpreted as affecting the probability that a 1 is output at that node. In particular, $\Phi^P(v_i)$ is the probability that $\Phi(v_i) = 1$.

In equational form, the output of a 3-state PLN is determined by

$$\Phi^P(v_0) = \Phi^P(0) = 0$$

$$\Phi^P(v_1) = \Phi^P(u) = 0.5 \qquad \text{or simply,} \quad \Phi^P(v_i) = \frac{i}{2} \qquad (3.27)$$

$$\Phi^P(v_2) = \Phi^P(1) = 1.0$$

In a ω-state PLN, typically one element of the stored value alphabet Ω, v_u, assumes the role of u, so that $\Phi(v_u) = 1$ with probability of $\frac{1}{2}$. Two possible Φ^P are

$$\Phi_S^P(v_i) = \frac{i}{\omega - 1}$$

$$\Phi_H^P(v_i) = 1, \qquad \text{if } i > u$$
$$= 0.5, \qquad \text{if } i = u$$
$$= 0, \qquad \text{if } i < u \qquad (3.28)$$

Φ_S^P is a step function approximating a linear output function. Because of the mutual independence of the stored values $loc_j[add_j]$ within a single node, the PLN is not restricted to linear functions, and may execute any arbitrary (non-monotonic, non-smooth, non-differentiable, etc.) output function. Φ_H^P is a step function which approximates a very steep sigmoidal curve. These two, Φ_S^P and Φ_H^P, may be viewed as creating maximally different output functions: the first is very 'soft' – if $i \approx j$, then $\Phi_S^P(i) \approx \Phi_S^P(j)$; the second is

---

[1] Kan (1988) has designed a 3-stage PLN system to maintain low I, and hence low memory requirements, but increase specificity and therefore memory capacity. He achieves this by transforming non-orthogonal inputs to address a different node location for each different output required. No disruption of previously trained states by new conflicting ones then occurs, since every new write is only made to a location not previously addressed. In specific, he amplifies the Hamming distance between patterns, using layers of nodes which repeatedly generate new addresses after a fashion not unlike hashing. After a few layers, similar inputs become quite differentiated in Hamming terms, and thus can be stored without conflict.

'hard' – $\Phi_H^P(v_{u-1})$ is maximally different from $\Phi_H^P(v_{u+1})$. Of course there exist an infinite number of curves between these two extremes which Φ^P may approximate.

A likely criterion for choice of Φ^P is its effect on the speed of convergence of the network. Myers (1989) shows theoretically and experimentally that speed can be maximized under certain conditions when Φ^P approximates a very steep sigmoid. Wong and Sherrington (1989) also show that with a steep Φ^P, and with $\omega = 11$, the net is much more robust with respect to training noise than it is at lower ω, and also that there is a greater storage capacity.

The result is intuitively satisfying: it suggests that once a node location is 'committed' to an output, i.e., that it has been reinforced even once away from v_u and toward 0 or 1, it should output that value consistently. This allows other locations in the net to organize around one another with some confidence that all are behaving as they expect to behave when fully trained.

It is also possible to anneal a PLN system. This would involve 'cooling' the system by gradually changing from a linear Φ^P to a steep one. This has the same effect as changing from a high temperature (high noise) to a low one (low noise) in a weighted-sum-and-threshold system. It is to be expected that this strategy, like for weighted-sum-and-threshold nodes, would help avoid the system settling into local minima, but that it would take an extremely long convergence time.

3.6.3 ω – the cardinality of the stored value alphabet

The final major variable in the PLN is Ω, the alphabet of possible stored values, or simply ω, the cardinality of Ω.

The advantage of $\omega > 3$ (and thus of the ω-state PLN over the 3-state PLN) is that after several reinforcements of a $loc_j[add_j]$ in one direction – so $loc_j[add_j]$ stores v_i where $i \approx 0$ or $i \approx \omega - 1$ – it can be hard to erase that knowledge: in fact, it will take an equal number of negative experiences to return it to v_u. Errors may occur due to mis-set stored values elsewhere in the net, but during which $loc_j[add_j]$ happens to be addressed, and $loc_j[add_j]$ will be negatively reinforced since the error signal is global and indiscriminate. If ω is high, and v_i is far from v_u, $loc_j[add_j]$ will be pushed back towards v_u but only by $1/\omega$, and the probability of outputting a 1 when $loc_j[add_j]$ is addressed need only change very little – particularly if Φ^P is a steep sigmoid. In a network where $\omega = 3$, in contrast, as discussed above, a single error arising anywhere in the net results in one location in each node being reset to v_u, and thus a great deal of knowledge is erased, regardless of whether any individual node is responsible for the error.

Increasing ω has its costs. The first is that an order of $\log_2 \omega$ bits will be required to store each $v_i \in \Omega$, making the RAM needed in each node scale as $2^I \log_2 \omega$. The expression is exponential in I, the number of inputs to the node, and this may dominate the cost for moderate ω.

Also, with a $loc_j[add_j]$ which stores v_i where $i \approx 0$ or $i \approx \omega - 1$, high ω means that it will be very difficult to return $loc_j[add_j]$ to v_u when this is required. Noisy data or unfortunate ordering of training examples could push a location's value very far from v_u, and an equal number of error cycles will be required to reset it.

Ideally, ω must be chosen to balance protection against mistaken erasure versus ability to erase when this becomes necessary. Myers (1989) indicates that an ω larger than 3, but still relatively small, leads to good convergence speed: in particular, the rule $5 \leqslant \omega \leqslant 15$ is suggested. Experiments reported there support this result: for example, on several problems nets with $\omega = 11$ converge faster than nets with $\omega = 6$ or $\omega = 20$.

3.6.4 PLN parameters – conclusions

Several assumptions are implicit in the choice of Φ_H^P and $\omega \approx 11$. The analyses consider feedforward pyramids, being trained on problems for which convergence is possible, via a training schedule which involves a random ordering of training patterns. This is a constrained class of topology and task, but one which is still quite powerful.

Given these assumptions, a ω-state PLN net may be designed which will tend to converge as fast as possible: namely, its nodes contain stored values selected from a 5–15 element alphabet, and which are interpreted according to a threshold-like output function. The experiments described in support of these claims (Myers, 1989) are small both in terms of the number of nodes involved and also in terms of the size of state space relative to the number of solutions available. They are useful however since a small number of distinguishable solutions exist and since the parity problem in particular is arguably the 'hardest' of the hard learning problems.

It is not the case that any ω and Φ^P are universally optimal: it is not clear in the first place that speed of convergence is a necessary criterion to judge the 'success' of a network – although it is probably the most frequent. There are occasions when a soft output function, for example, will be desirable despite its slowness. One obvious example involves a state space with abundant and deep local minima (false solutions), where probabilistic noisy outputs are necessary; in effect, a network using a steep output function forms quick and binding opinions, whereas a network with a more linear output function makes conservative ones, which still allow occasional lapses into the opposite output. This ability would prove important in a changing environment, where convergence per se is not possible, and where a net might be more successful if some of its nodes, say, output a 1 most of the time and occasionally output a 0 to test the effects in the current environment.

Appropriate choice of parameters is therefore highly dependent on the size, shape and complexity of the problem space, and also causes subtle changes in the way the net organizes to solve the problem – particularly in terms of the speed with which nodes commit to a particular output in response to some addresses. No values of ω and Φ^p can therefore be purported to be optimal under all conditions, merely especially useful, and good first approximations for later fine-tuning as necessary.

3.7 RAM-based nodes: biological connections

A frequent objection to the use of RAM-based nodes instead of weight-using nodes is that they seem to sacrifice biological plausibility in favour of an engineering solution. In computational applications, this is probably irrelevant; but there remains a feeling among sections of the connectionist community that "if it hasn't got weights, it isn't a neural network". This distrust seems to stem from the idea that adjusting real-valued weights on connections between summing units is somehow a more biologically valid metaphor than adjusting look-up table contents.

However, there are several compelling arguments why RAM-based nodes are, in fact, relevant to modelling of biological systems.

An important result, proven by Gorse and Taylor (1988), is that networks of noisy RAM-nodes have functional equivalence to networks of noisy neurons. Taylor has developed a noisy neural model (Taylor, 1972; Gorse, 1989), which considers N arbitrarily connected neurons j, each with probability $p_j(t)$ of firing at time t. The firing at t is determined by the total amount of transmitters received by j, in which the presynaptic neuron releases transmitters according to a Poisson process, which includes both spontaneous and presynaptic-dependent components. The evolvement through time of a network of these units can then be computed. Taylor goes on to show (Gorse and Taylor, 1988) that a pRAM network can implement the noisy neural network, and that, with a few constraints, "the dynamical behaviour of any net of noisy neurons can be mirrored by that of some net of pRAMs, and vice versa."

This result is the equivalent, for RAM-based nodes, of the McCulloch and Pitts (1943) assertion for threshold logic units.

At a slightly higher level, the information-processing level, there is also good reason to consider the biological relevance of RAM-based nodes.

Purkinje neurons in cerebellar cortex are involved in the learning and expression of conditioned responses such as the blink of a rabbit's nictitating membrane (third eyelid) in response to a puff of air. Each Purkinje receives approximately 200,000 synapses on its distal dendrites; the cells have 'active zones' which can include space-limited action potentials. One implication of the dendritic layout is that large dendrites may act to perform a logical AND (multiplication) or a logical OR (addition) on its input from the smaller dendritic branches which merge onto it. This implies that the cells are capable of integrating high-order combinations of their inputs (Durbin and Rumelhart, 1989). In a computational model, this corresponds to providing not only the values of the current I inputs, but also values of various combinations of inputs. If every possible combination is implemented, the result is a RAM-node; if combinations of various numbers of inputs are considered, the result is an i-pRAM (Clarkson *et al.*, 1991).

At an even higher level, that of computational modelling, higher order combinations of inputs are also important. Stimulus–response learning is often modelled by the Rescorla–Wagner (1972) learning rule, which is functionally equivalent to the LMS rule (Widrow and Hoff, 1960)

$$\Delta w_{ji} = \beta(t_j - y_j)x_i \qquad (3.29)$$

This treats each input x_i as a line with an adjustable weight; through training, the node j learns which inputs are significant and should tend to produce output activity. However, there are several conditioning phenomena which this model does not address.

One important example is negative patterning, the conditioning version of the exclusive-or problem. Here, the animal must learn that stimulus A alone or stimulus B alone signals the appearance of a reinforcer, but that A and B presented together do not. Gluck and Bower (1988) showed that animal and human classification behaviour is better matched by a 'configural cue' model, which allows weights not only to individual cues, but to higher order combinations of cues. Again, this is a good reason to consider the RAM-based node, which inherently involves these higher order configurations.

A developing hypothesis in connectionist research is that, if a problem is solvable by some topology of some kind of node, then it is also possible to solve the problem with any other kind of node in some topology – given such constraints as binary/continuous input and comparable training paradigms exist. On this assumption, it makes sense to choose a model which solves a given problem in a manner which is accurate, fast and easy to implement. In many cases, this seems to argue for the use of a RAM-based node.

Accordingly, the machines described in the chapters which follow are based on such nodes – specifically the ω-state PLN.

4

Attention-driven buffering

One way of classifying the delay learning systems discussed in Chapter 2 is as 'forward-looking' or 'backward-looking'. In the former, the time frame centres on a potential action, and predicts what will happen in the future if that action is in fact carried out. In the latter, the time frame centres on a received reinforcement, and involves remembering the sequence of actions which preceded it. Systems which use temporal differences are forward-looking; those using buffers or eligibility traces are backward-looking.

Forward-looking systems have an advantage of being applicable to a wide range of difficult learning problems, as described in Chapter 2; they also have a certain elegance in seeming to make intelligent guesses about future consequences. But they sacrifice much of the information available to history-maintaining systems, and accordingly can still be shown to be unable to solve problems where previous states influence the outcome of an action in the current state.

An attractive compromise would be a system capable of both forward- and backward-looking features: one which predicts the future results of actions and also keeps a memory of past actions with which to associate reinforcement when it arrives.

The method of attention-driven buffering, ADB (Myers, 1990, 1991a), is an instantiation of such a compromise. An ADB system maintains a buffer of n past input–output pairs, but those n patterns are selected according to **attention** rather than strictly according to closeness in time.

Attention is a familiar concept in cognitive psychology describing human learning. Eysenck (1984), for example, argues that we "choose to attend to" sources of information which are relevant to our current goals, which have species-specific meaning, or which are *novel, incongruous or surprising*. The concept of attention also features in the work of Grossberg and Carpenter with unsupervised neural networks: in their systems, if an input pattern is sufficiently unlike any known prototype, an **attentional reset** occurs, signalling that there is a novel input to which the system does not know how to respond (Grossberg, 1980; Carpenter and Grossberg, 1988).

Within ADB, attention is likewise indicated when the inputs are novel or surprising. It is formally defined as the 'uncertainty that a particular action will elicit a particular reinforcement'. If an action output in response to an input pattern is well-known to result in reinforcement r, then the attention to that pattern will be low, and it will be unlikely to be buffered. If the result of an action is unknown, and the system effectively 'guesses' in choosing it, attention will be high, and the input–output pair will make a strong bid for buffer space. Once in the buffer, attention decays with time. Therefore, the buffer represents a memory storing the n most recent, most unpredictable input–output pairs occurring. This means that, although the buffer size is fixed at n, the system can learn about actions with reinforcement delayed more than n time steps, since each intervening pattern is not automatically stored. This overcomes many of the short-comings of temporal differences, eligibilities and buffers used on their own.

The ADB system is forward-looking because, in addition to predicting the results of actions, it also judges the confidence with which it makes that prediction; yet it can be shown to overcome the chief difficulty of temporal difference learning: namely, inability to learn to respond differently to patterns which always occur close together in time – section 4.2 will show an example of this. The ADB system is also backward-looking because it maintains explicit information about past states with which to associate reinforcement when it arrives; yet it can also overcome the basic short-comings of simple buffering or eligibility-maintaining systems: namely that since reinforcement will be associated with *every* stored pattern and because of space constraints limiting buffer size, only small amounts of recent information may be kept in the buffer or in the eligibility traces, but this conflicts with the need to learn associations which involve indefinitely long delays.

4.1 The ADB approach

An ADB system, like other exploratory and reinforcement learning systems, interacts with an environment or world, as shown in Figure 2.2; but it contains several components. Figure 4.1 illustrates these components: namely, a learning system or neural network, output-generating and attention-setting mechanisms, and a buffer.

Input to the system from the world passes to the learning system. The simplest form this can take is a series of neural networks which each vote for an output or action for the system to take, based on their individual past experience. Each of these votes passes to a system output generator, which determines the single action undertaken. Another module determines the attention assigned to this input – action pair: for example, setting attention as a function of how many of the networks voiced dissenting opinions. The selected action is the output of the ADB system to the world.

To satisfy the demands of delay learning, the system must be able to cope

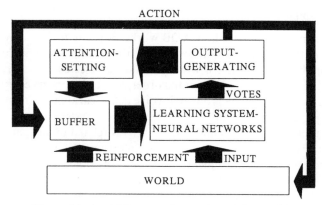

Figure 4.1 *An ADB system interacting with a world.*

when reinforcement signals from the world are delayed and interleaved with other feedback. To accomplish this, a buffer is provided within the system to store past states (input-output pairs) until reinforcement arrives. Because the buffer is of bounded size and yet delays may be indefinitely long, past states are not kept indiscriminately. Instead, the entry of states into the buffer is governed by the attention assigned to each state. This attention is at a minimum when all neural networks vote for the same action, and at a maximum when there is dissension and the action is randomly selected from among them. If the attention assigned to the current state is higher than that of at least one presently buffered state, that state is ousted and its place is taken by the current state, together with its attention. With each time step that a state remains in the buffer, its attention decays toward zero.

When reinforcement arrives from the world, each state in the buffer is examined. For each state with non-zero attention, the buffered input pattern is reapplied to the learning system, and the buffered output is reinforced positively or negatively, as the reinforcement signal indicates. This will encourage or discourage each neural network to vote to repeat that output action when next the input pattern appears.

The result is a system which compromises between forward-looking and backward-looking delay learning paradigms. It keeps a buffer of size n, but can store a state for more than n cycles if attention is sufficiently high. It assigns reinforcement to states based on recency, in the sense that attention decays with time, but unlike strictly eligibility-based systems, the reinforcement to a state s is not necessarily related to the reinforcement to the states which preceded it or followed it – because these states may not be in the buffer when s is reinforced. And it makes use of a simple form of prediction, in terms of confidence in future reinforcement, but unlike temporal difference systems it makes a start at separating continuity in time from contingency.

4.2 An example

A small example illustrates how ADB works. Suppose the task involves, for instance, outputting a decision to 'accept' all of the patterns in Figure 4.2, except for the final X pattern which should be 'rejected'. The patterns are presented to the network in sequential order, so that X appears every eleventh time step. And to make the problem involve delay learning, the reinforcement schedule provides results three time steps after the system outputs an accept response to a pattern. No reinforcement arrives related to any pattern which was rejected; the system receives negative reinforcement if the accepted pattern was X and positive reinforcement if it accepts any other pattern. The system might be implementing a 'bug' which, instead of learning to locomote, is learning what is suitable to eat in a world where most things are tasty, one kind is not, and there is no effect at all from something which is passed over and not eaten.

Finally, to illustrate the point that an ADB system can learn even when the delay to reinforcement is longer than n, the buffer size is set at $n = 3$. This means that, without the use of attention-driven buffering, the three intervening patterns would have filled the buffer, ousting the pattern with which reinforcement should be associated, by the time that reinforcement arrives.

The neural networks for this task, as in all ADB experiments described within this book are based on the ω-state PLNs defined in the previous chapter. However, it should be stressed from the onset that the concept of attention-driven buffering is independent of the node model used in the learning system. In fact, the basic idea of ADB would still work even if the learning system were implemented via, for example, a rule-based approach.

The PLNs used here are specifically instantiated by the rules

$$loc_j[add_j] \in \{0.00, 0.01, 0.02, \ldots, 1.00\} \tag{4.1}$$

$$\Phi(x) = 1 \qquad \text{with probability } x \tag{4.2}$$

Training followed the reinforcement learning rule (Myers and Aleksander, 1988)

$$\Delta loc_j[add_j] = \text{sign } (y_j - 0.5)\beta^r \tag{4.3}$$

(with loc_j bounded at 0.0 and 1.0), upon receipt of reinforcement $r \in \{-, 0, +\}$.

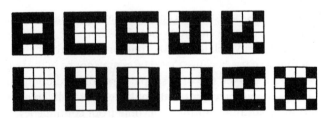

Figure 4.2 *Example training set, all to be 'accepted' except the last X pattern.*

For this experiment, $\beta^0 = 0.0$, $\beta^+ = 0.05$, while $\beta^- = -0.25$; the negative increment β^- is larger in magnitude than β^+ because in this task, negative reinforcement is much more infrequent, especially as learning proceeds.

Because the association problem defined by Figure 4.2 is not too difficult (only the reinforcement schedule complicates it), each 'neural network' in the learning system is composed of a single PLN; the learning system consists of 20 of these, each with four inputs, and each therefore sampling a random 25% of the 16-bit input space. The output of this system is the sum of the 20 outputs, and therefore a vote tally in the range $0 \leqslant V \leqslant 20$.

This vote tally then feeds into the output-generator and the attention-setting mechanism. The output generator follows the simple rule

$$output = accept \text{ iff } V \geqslant 18 \qquad (4.4)$$

This threshold of 18 was chosen in accordance with heuristics, but full discussion of these heuristics is delayed until the next chapter.

The attention-setting mechanism $att = f(x)$ implements an approximation to a bell curve, as shown in Figure 4.3; with each time step spent in the buffer, attention decays by $att \leftarrow att - \delta$, where $\delta = 0.1$. The system is considered to have successfully solved the problem when 5,000 time steps (or about 455 sweeps through the 11-pattern training set) elapse without negative reinforcement. (This 5,000 step interval is discounted in subsequent calculations of learning times).

The results of a series of experiments with this system are shown in Figure 4.4, and show that over half of the systems tested could learn the problem within less than 1,000 time steps. A few took significantly longer. An alternative measure of learning speed is the number of negative reinforcements encountered overall, and this averaged 21.3.

In this task, patterns A, C, and F were always more recent than X when the negative reinforcement elicited by an acceptance of X arrived. In a system which buffered purely on the basis of recency, therefore, F would become most strongly associated with negative reinforcement, and C, A, and X progressively less so. If the buffer size was $n = 3$, as in the current system, X would in fact never become associated with the negative reinforcement arriving at a delay of $D = 3$.

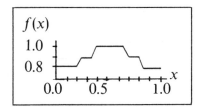

Figure 4.3 *The attention-setting function for the problem of Figure 4.2.*

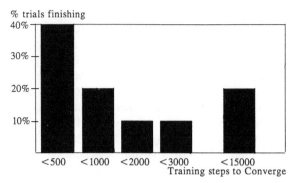

Figure 4.4 *Time steps to convergence on problem of Figure 4.2, average of 10 ADB systems.*

Using an ADB system, it is possible to learn that A, C, and F are actually unrelated to the arrival of negative reinforcement. In fact, over half of the ten systems generating the results in Figure 4.4 successfully learned to reject X but to accept all other patterns. Not all learned to accept all of the positive patterns, however: some failed to recognize that patterns which always appeared close in time to negative reinforcement could be positive. In fact, 40% of the nets shown in Figure 4.4 learned to reject one or more positive patterns from the training set. (In all, the average number of positives accepted by the systems was 9.1 of 10 – or an average of just less than one falsely rejected.) While such behaviour still satisfies the single criterion of avoiding negative reinforcement, it does not maximize positive reinforcement.

Optimal behaviour can be defined as behaviour which maximizes positive while minimizing negative reinforcement to the system. In the context of this task, it involves consistent rejection of the X pattern and consistent acceptance of *all* other patterns – even those which always precede or trail X in the presentation sequence. One way of increasing the likelihood of this result is by increasing n, the buffer size. This allows each state to remain in the buffer for longer, and since the reinforcements experienced are predominantly positive, each pattern will be associated with more positive reinforcements.

Figure 4.5 shows some results of the same ADB system as described above, but with varying n and with acceptance occurring when more than 18 nodes vote for an accept action by outputting $y_j = 1$. The figure shows that, in fact, the number of positives rejected does decrease with increasing n, as predicted. It also shows that training time, both in terms of time steps and in terms of negative reinforcements received, falls as n increases. The negative pattern X is learned faster because, with larger n, it is more likely to still be resident in the buffer when the negative reinforcement arrives. The positive patterns are learned more quickly because, with larger n, each stays in the buffer longer; since most time steps bring positive reinforcement, each is associated with

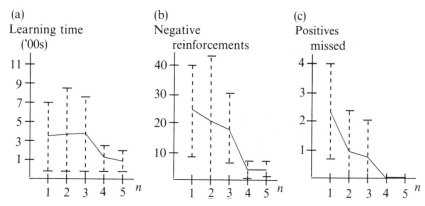

Figure 4.5 *Influence of buffer size n on (a) learning time, (b) negative reinforcements before learning completed, (c) average positive patterns rejected after learning completed. Each point is average of 20 ADB systems; vertical bars show one standard deviation, from Myers (1991a).*

more positive reinforcement during each stay in the buffer. A final important point to notice about the results in Figure 4.5 is that *even with buffer size as low as $n = 1$,* the problem is still learnable. More negative reinforcements are required before learning, and the final solution involves more positives rejected on average, but the system can still learn to avoid negative patterns when reinforcement is delayed.

4.3 The location of the buffer

So far, the system has been described as keeping a buffer which is accessory to the learning system, and which maintains external input and output patterns. It is equally possible to maintain buffers at the level of individual nodes. That is, each node j could buffer its own selection of n recent inputs $(x_{j1}, x_{j2}, \ldots, x_{jl})$ each paired with the vote y_{jl} it output in response.

Figure 4.6a shows an ADB system implemented with external buffering. Each input pattern passes through the neural network, and is eventually assigned an attention if action is taken. If this attention is greater than some state in the external buffer, the current input, action and attention replace that state. On reinforcement, each input pattern stored in the buffer with non-zero attention is reapplied to the neural network. Each node in the memory takes its input from this pattern and is reinforced accordingly. The space required for an external buffer scales as $n(B + k)$, for buffer size n, a B-bit external input pattern, and an attention coded in k bits.

A system with internal buffering is shown in Figure 4.6b. Here, the nodes consist of (for example) I-input PLNs each augmented with its own buffer of n, $(I + k)$-bit states. Once attention is calculated, each node compares this new

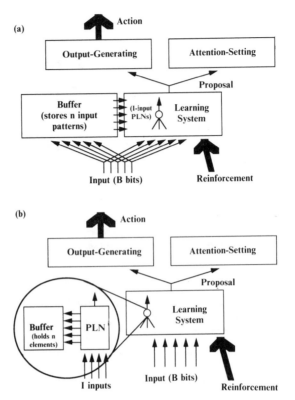

Figure 4.6 *An ADB system with (a) external or (b) internal buffers.*

attention with those of the states in its internal buffer; if the new attention is higher than some resident state, a new state is constructed of the current I node inputs and the new attention, and this overwrites the resident state. Reinforcement causes each node to reapply the I-bit buffered patterns with non-zero attention to its input lines, and update accordingly. Space requirements for an N-node net will be $Nn(I + k)$; for nets where $B < NI$ (for example multi-layered nets or nets where bits of the input pattern feed into more than one bottom-layer node), the space required will be considerably larger than for the system with external buffering.

By maintaining an internal buffer at the node level (rather than externally at the system level), updates – putting states into the buffer and also retrieving them and reinforcing the nodes – may be done locally and therefore the operation is massively parallel. If the updates are done on a system-wide level, the operation can only be parallel within a layer, and therefore in the best case, time complexity will be related to the number of layers in the neural network. Another potential feature might be that each network could calculate attention individually: for example, one node which made a very confident decision to output a vote might assign lower attention to the input if the system output was in accordance with the action it voted for, but very high attention if system output differed. This would require redefinition of the criteria determining attention-assignment.

While the implementation would not necessarily be trivial, it is an encouraging feature of the ADB model that it can be implemented in this massively parallel, local and distributed fashion.

For the remainder of this book, mention will generally be made of 'the buffer' to simplify discussion; such usage does not preclude the existence of many internal buffers in the actual implementation. In fact, because the neural networks in the ADB systems described throughout this book will be single-layer, there is functional equivalence between external and internal buffering.

4.4 An example 'bug'

The preceding sections of this chapter have described the design of a system which is exploratory, which requires only a scalar reinforcement signal, and which can extrapolate from results which occur only at the end of a series of actions.

An example situation in which such behaviour is required is the class of 'bug' problems. As mentioned earlier, these involve simulated creatures which roam a two-dimensional world, seeking food and possibly avoiding predators. In addition to the Cecconi–Parisi system described in Chapter 2, bugs have been studied by a number of neural network researchers. For example, Ackley and Littman (1990) studied a bug trained by reinforcement learning and existing in a complex environment containing such objects as multiple autonomous bugs, ambulatory predators, impassable walls, and sheltering trees. Their creatures then spawned according to a genetic algorithm; and after several generations creatures evolved which managed to survive for more than one million time steps. Patarnello and Carnevalli (1990) considered a bug containing a neural network of fixed-function RAM-nodes which learned by optimizing over connections between nodes, and with only binary external input: indicating if the bug was facing food and if there was food on an adjoining location. In an approach not involving neural networks, Doran (1968) used a rule-based learning system to implement a bug which learned to find its way back to a burrow.

The variant of the problem considered here involves a world which is better described as a labyrinth than as a two-dimensional grid. That is, as the bug moves from location to location, knowledge of the current location can be used to predict future ones, in a manner which is impossible if the world consists of a number of food objects scattered at random across a grid. The bug finds putative food objects at each location, but at some locations, the object is edible while at other locations the object will make the bug 'sick'; the objective is to maximize food eaten while minimizing sickness.

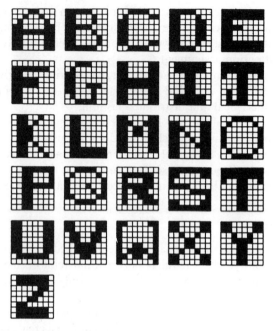

Figure 4.7 *Inputs to the ADB bug representing locations, after Myers (1991a) with patterns designed by E. Fulcher (1991).*

A set M of world locations exists, each location providing a distinct 64-bit input pattern to the system, as shown in Figure 4.7. Of these some $M^- \in M$ are negative (specifically patterns A, B and C) while the remainder $M^+ = M - M^-$ are positive. At each time step, the bug is in some location $\mu_t \in M$, and can output a decision $m_t \in \{L, R, A\}$ to move left, right or straight ahead. The labyrinth is defined so that the next location follows the rule: $\mu_{t+1} = g(\mu_t, m_t)$. If $\mu_{t+1} \in M^-$, there is an immediate positive reinforcement followed by a negative reinforcement four time steps later – as if the bug ate something which later made it mildly sick. The rules by which the bug moves from one location to the next are shown in Figure 4.8. (They are designed so that no location leads to itself, or else a legal solution would be for the bug to enter a positive location and then remain permanently there!)

Thus the bug's task is first to learn to predict the three labyrinth locations which adjoin the current one μ_t, and second to select the moves which result in entering an adjoining location $\mu_{t+1} \in M^+$, even though negative results are delayed and contradictory signals may intervene. For example, negative reinforcement may not arrive until some time after $\mu_t \in M^-$ was entered and may arrive just after some location in M^+ has been entered. After learning, all negative locations should be transient; that is, the system should never execute a move which leads to a negative location. As many as possible of the positive

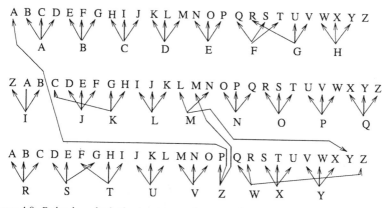

Figure 4.8 *Rules by which the bug moves from one location to the next; for example, moving left, ahead or right from location I leads to locations Z, A or B, respectively.*

locations should be re-entrant: that is, the bug should be disposed to enter positive locations when a move from the current one leads there.

There are many complications. Locations such as R which are themselves positive but which lead in turn only to negative locations should be avoided. Locations such as I, K and Z, from which one or more moves lead to a negative location, should be re-entrant as long as there is at least one possible move leading from them to a positive location. Locations often entered after a negative one, such as D, E and J should not themselves be associated with negative reinforcement just because there may be negative reinforcement which arrives soon after they are entered.

The ADB system used to solve this problem is shown in Figure 4.9. It consists of two separate learning modules. One, the **associator module**, simply learns to predict the next location if a particular move is made from the current location. A second, **judge module**, used ADB techniques to assess likely future reinforcement if that predicted next location is entered.

The associator module faces a task which does not involve delay learning. Rather, it should come to execute a straightforward mapping

$$\mu_{t+1} \in M = \phi[\mu_t \in M, m_t \in \{L, R, A\}] \qquad (4.5)$$

Ideally ϕ should be identical to the rules shown in Figure 4.8. The module was implemented as a PLN network consisting of 64 pyramid structures. A pyramid is a network of nodes in which each output feeds into exactly one higher layer node. By this definition, the network contains progressively fewer nodes at each layer, until the output layer consists of a single node – giving the network its pyramidal appearance. In the associator module, the 64 pyramids and associated 64 outputs could therefore be trained to provide an estimate of the input pattern predicted to appear at time $t + 1$ given the current location and move.

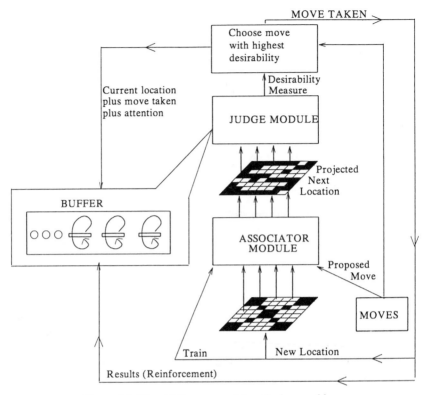

Figure 4.9 *The ADB system solving the bug problem.*

Each pyramid contains at its bottom layer eight PLNs, which each receive input from two bits encoding a potential move m_t and eight bits mapped randomly from the current input pattern describing μ_t. The input pattern is thus completely covered, as each bit is mapped to exactly one PLN in the pyramid. The eight bottom-layer PLNs feed into a single second layer node for each pyramid: the output node for that pyramid. All values stored at all locations in all nodes in all pyramids are initialized to 0.5. The output is generated by the rule

$$y_j = \Phi(loc_j[add_j]) \qquad (4.6)$$

where

$$\begin{aligned}
&\text{if } x < 0.5 \quad \Phi(x) = 0 \\
&\text{if } x > 0.5 \quad \Phi(x) = 1 \\
&\text{if } x = 0.5 \quad \Phi(x) = 0 \text{ or } 1 \text{ with equal probability}
\end{aligned}$$

This rule was justified by Myers (1989) as providing fast learning: as soon as a node begins to commit itself to outputting a certain output response to an input pattern, by incrementing $loc_j[add_j]$ away from the initial value 0.5, the output is no longer subject to fluctuations as it would be if the rule '$\Phi(x) = 1$ with probability x' were used.

At each time step t, a move m_{t-1} is executed, and the new location μ_t is computed. At this point the last location μ_t is clamped as output, and each node j in the network is simply trained as

$$\Delta loc_j[add_j] = 10 \, \text{sign} \, (0.5 - t_j) \qquad \text{if } t_j = d_j$$
$$= -10 \, \text{sign} \, (0.5 - t_j) \qquad \text{if } t_j \neq d_j \qquad (4.7)$$

where t_j is the value output by the topmost node in the pyramid to which j belongs, and d_j is the bit in the pattern representing μ_j which j's pyramid is to learn to predict.

It is in the judge module that the concepts of reinforcement learning and delay learning are applied. When the bug enters a location μ_t, the associator module produces each of the three input patterns it predicts will appear if the bug moves left, right or ahead. The judge module processes each of these predicted next locations in turn, and outputs a desirability rating for each. The system as a whole then outputs the move m_t which the modules together predicted would result in the highest desirability rating.

The judge module is an ADB system. Its learning system consists of a single layer of 25 8-input PLNs (and so every bit in the module's input is mapped 3–4 times), with every location in each node initialized to 0.5, and which use the output rule $y_j = 1$ with probability equal to $loc_j[add_j]$. The desirability rating of the input pattern is then the sum of the judge module nodes which output 1 in response, and is a number in the range 0–25.

The output generating module then selects the move m_t for which the predicted next location μ_t^* (output by the associator module) generated the highest desirability in the judge module.

The predicted next location μ_t^* is stored in the ADB buffer ($n = 5$), where attention is set as $f(x) = 1.0$, and is decremented by $\delta = 0.2$. When results $r \in \{-, 0, +\}$ arrive, the judge module is trained so that each location in the buffer is reapplied as input, and the PLNs within the judge module are updated as

$$\Delta loc_j[add_j] = \beta^r \qquad \text{if } y_j = 1$$
$$= -\beta^r \qquad \text{if } y_j = 0 \qquad (4.8)$$

As usual, $\beta^0 = 0.0$, $\beta^+ = 0.05$, while $\beta^- = 0.25$. This ensures that, if reinforcement is positive, desirability will rise; while it will fall if reinforcement is negative. Again, the negative increment is larger since there are fewer negative than positive locations in M.

The full system is trained by allowing the bug to roam the labyrinth, receiving appropriate reinforcements as well as learning which locations follow from what moves, until learning is such that the negative locations would never again be entered. This can be determined from observing the desirabilities assigned to each possible next location. Since the system will always move to the next location with the highest desirability, it suffices that for each location μ_t in which it is possible to enter a negative location μ_N by executing move m_N, there is also at least one move m_P which would result in entering a positive location μ_P and which has a higher desirability than μ_N. It must also be the case that if a location exists which leads only to negative locations (location R, in this case), that that location also have a low enough desirability that it will never be entered.

Experimentally, the system tends to find solutions in which no negative state is re-entrant, within about 2,000 time steps or 24 negative reinforcements (Myers, 1991a). However, as in the examples of section 4.2, not every positive location is necessarily re-entrant. This does not imply that desirabilities for these locations were as low as, say, those of the negative locations; but merely that in every location from which they could be reached, at least one other move was available leading to a (positive) location with still higher desirability. Figure 4.10a shows one such solution: no negative state is re-entrant, and neither is state R, and the solution therefore fills the criteria. This system entered negative locations 22 times within the first 1,000 time steps, then only entered one more negative location within the next 3,000 time steps; after that, desirabilities were set such that no negative state would be re-entrant. However, positive states D, E, G, K, N, E and W were also not re-entrant.

An alternate strategy for training this system is to train the associator module first and separately to predict next locations, and then train the judge module after to generate high desirability for moves leading to positive next locations. This means that the judge module will be getting accurate predictions from the start: ordinarily, it is trying to learn desirability ratings for associator module output while the associator module is still trying to stabilize

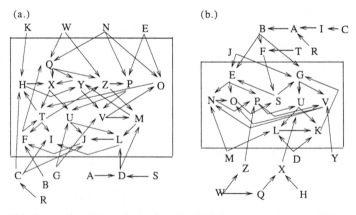

Figure 4.10 *Example solutions found by the ADB bug (a) with both modules trained together, and (b) with pre-trained associator module. The re-entrant states are enclosed within the box; from Myers (1991a).*

its own predictions. Under these modified learning conditions, the system learns faster. For example, the associator module can learn perfect predictions within 2,000 time steps (in which it is presented with random current locations and moves together with the location which would result). Following that, the judge module can learn to avoid all negative locations within a mere 500 time steps' worth of wandering through the labyrinth.

However, the increased learning speed is achieved at a cost. Figure 4.10b shows one example solution found by a system with separately-trained modules. Although the solution meets the criteria that states A, B, C and R are not re-entrant, it also leaves 12 of the remaining 22 positive states transient. The reason for this behaviour is that because learning proceeds so quickly, the system quickly settles into deterministic behaviour, finding a cycle (such as L–K–G–V–N–O–S–E–P–U–L... in Figure 4.10b) which consists wholly of positive locations. It then has no reason to deviate from this cycle ever again. On the other hand, in the case when the two modules are trained together, the judge module by virtue of its imperfect input will make imperfect desirability ratings, and it is much more likely that the bug will deviate from this kind of cycle. Because it explores more locations within the labyrinth, it will learn that more locations are positive (and should have a high desirability rating). This results in a broader spectrum of available moves in Figure 4.10a than in Figure 4.10b.

4.5 Comparison with other delay learning methods

Attention-driven buffering is a method for allowing a neural network to be trained in a reinforcement learning paradigm, even when the reinforcement may be delayed in time such that other events and even reinforcements may arrive in the interim. These conditions define delay learning.

The bug example of the previous section and the examples of section 4.2 are fairly simple tasks as far as pattern association: they contain relatively few patterns to be learned, each involves unique and predictable reinforcements, and in the case of the bug, the rules governing movement within the labyrinth are deterministic and hence perfectly learnable. It is the delay learning feature of the tasks that makes them non-trivial.

Clearly, simple (reinforcement-learning) neural networks would be unable to learn the bug problem. A system in which a teacher mapped the tasks onto non-temporal problems would have been able to perform well, but this approach has already been dismissed as lacking sufficient generality as a method of delay learning. A system which maintained buffers would also have been able to learn the bug problem, given that its buffer size n was larger than the maximum possible interval between action and reinforcement. However, it would then fail to learn an identical problem in which the delay was increased as little as to $n + 1$: again this is therefore not a sufficiently general solution. Systems using the methods of eligibility traces and temporal differences would have been able to deal with the tasks even with indefinite extension of the delay. The difficulty with these systems is, as has been explained, that they associate the reinforcement obtained from some state μ_t with μ_{t-1} and μ_{t+1} as well. Therefore, in the problem of section 4.2, where positive pattern A always followed negative pattern X and positive pattern Z always preceded it, temporal difference methods would have been categorically unable to learn that A and Z were positive.

In the bug example, since location H is sometimes entered after location C, and since location C is associated with negative reinforcement, temporal difference methods would assign to H some of the negative reinforcement. Yet location H is itself positive, and should instead rate a desirability as high as any other arbitrary positive state. In an ADB system this is possible. In fact, Figure 4.10a shows that location H has sufficient desirability to be re-entrant after training.

The chief short-coming of the ADB approach is also shown in Figure 4.10a: once a location, such as K, achieves a low enough desirability rating that its attention also drops dramatically, it will never again manage to enter the buffer. This means that the system will never learn anything more about location K, and it is impossible to retrieve the potential of learning that K is in fact a positive location. There are at least three ways in which this difficulty could be overcome. The first is that the attention-setting mechanism could ensure that attention never drops quite low enough to absolutely preclude an element's entry to the buffer. A second approach would be to include a probabilistic element in the output-generating module. In this way, every location like K would eventually be re-entered by the system. Once K was re-entered, and no ill-effects of negative reinforcement were encountered, the desirability rating of K would begin to increase. Because the system has a distributed memory, it is also possible that changes in the response to other patterns may affect the response to K as well – perhaps with the extra effect of raising K's desirability.

In the experiments described in this chapter, all of the parameters such as attention-setting function, output-generating routine, and selection of β^+, β^- and the other variables have been mentioned without any justification. The next chapter aims to provide a more formal account of how these variables influence the system, and to describe some heuristics which constrain their selection.

5

Analysis of parameters

This chapter proves several propositions about ADB systems, and provides a series of heuristics for the choice of parameters in constructing one. Readers not interested in formal proofs may wish to skip directly to section 5.6, which contains a summary of the heuristics produced.

The first order of business is a formal definition of an ADB system and the world or environment with which it interacts.

At each time t, the ADB system receives as input a pattern $P_i(t) \in M$ representing the current state i, and a series of zero or more reinforcements. Each reinforcement $c_{km}(t)$ scheduled to arrive at time t represents the response of the world when, at a previous time, the ADB system output a response a_k to its then-current input P_m. The ADB system updates its learning system on the basis of the c_{km}, and then produces output $a_j(t)$, one of a finite set of A possible outputs available

$$ADB: P_i(t) \times [c_{km}(t)] \to a_j(t), \qquad 1 \leqslant j, k \leqslant A, \quad 1 \leqslant i, m \leqslant |M| \qquad (5.1)$$

Internally, the ADB system consists of four conceptually basic modules: the learning system, the attention-setting mechanism, the output-generating system, and the buffer. (Physically, these may not be separate; as described in the last chapter, the buffer and attention-setting modules may be contained within the learning system, for example.)

The learning system must produce output which can be interpreted as a series of votes for each of the different output actions a_j available to the system. The most straightforward way in which this can be implemented is for the learning system to consist of a series of neural networks which each produce a vote for some action; these votes can then be summed to produce a strength of response favouring each possible action. Given input pattern $P_i(t)$, each possible action a_j is assigned a response equal to the sum of the networks voting for it $0 \leqslant V_{ji}(t) \leqslant V_{MAX}$, where V_{MAX} is the response if every neural network within the learning system votes for an action.

The initial response of the ADB system to a novel pattern P_i should be set so as to ensure that the system output is essentially a random response.

Ideally, this should be equal for any pattern P_i, at least in the initial stages of training; this initial response is given as $\hat{V}$.

The series $V_{ji}(t), 0 \leqslant j \leqslant A$, provides input to the output-generating module. There, a single action $a_j(t)$ is selected as the system output at time t. This may be done by choosing j to maximize $V_{ji}(t)$. Alternately, there may be a threshold ρ set so that if no other action satisfies the criterion $V_{ji}(t) \geqslant \rho$, then the output action is some default.

The vote tally $V_{ji}(t)$ associated with the output action $a_j(t)$ passes to the attention-setting mechanism. There, attention to the current input–output pair is generated

$$att_{ij}(t) = f(V_{ji}(t)), \qquad 0 \leqslant att_{ij}(t) \leqslant 1 \tag{5.2}$$

The attention-setting function f should satisfy the following conditions

$$f(\hat{V}) = 1.0 \tag{5.3}$$
$$\text{if } x < y \leqslant \hat{V}, \text{then } f(x) < f(y)$$
$$\text{if } x > y \geqslant \hat{V}, \text{then } f(x) < f(y)$$

That is, $f(x)$ should be non-decreasing to a maximum at $x = \hat{V}$ and non-increasing thereafter.

The generated attention $att_{ij}(t) = f(V_{ij}(t))$ governs the entry of the current input–output pair ($P_i(t)$ and $a_j(t)$) into the buffer. The buffer contains space for up to n states, each consisting of one such input–output pair and the associated attention. At time t, if some state in the buffer has attention $att_{km}(t) < att_{ij}(t)$, then the new state – consisting of the current input–output pair and $att_{ij}(t)$ – overwrites that state. At each time step, the attention of each state in the buffer is decremented as

$$att_{km}(t) = \max(att_{km}(t-1) - \delta, 0) \tag{5.4}$$

where $0 \leqslant \delta \leqslant 1.0$. Therefore, the maximum time a state can remain in the buffer with non-zero attention is $\lceil 1/\delta \rceil$.

A final aspect of the ADB system is how it updates according to the $c_{km}(t)$ arriving at time t. This is the first event at time t, even before new input $P_i(t)$ is attended to. If $c_{km}(t) \neq 0$, each state in the buffer is re-examined. If its attention is greater than zero, then the buffered input–output pair is reapplied to the learning system as input and output respectively, and each node in the network is updated according to a reinforcement learning rule based on $r = c_{km}(t)$. For a PLN j, the current address add_j is computed from the input pattern, and the learning rule would be

$$\Delta loc_j[add_j] = \text{sign}(y_j - 0.5)\beta^r \tag{5.5}$$

The node output y_j could either be buffered explicitly, generated anew by application of the node output function to the addressed stored value, or – in the case of a single layer net – approximated from the buffered system response a_j.

5.1 Reinforcement delay and buffer size

The examples in the last chapter showed that ADB systems with buffer size n are capable of learning even when the delay between output action and reinforcement exceeds n. This can also be shown formally for a simplified class of ADB systems. Specifically, the possible outputs of the system are restricted to $a_j \in \{0, 1\}$ $(A = 2)$, and the learning of a response to one pattern does not affect the response to any other pattern: the memories within the learning system should not interfere with each other. This system can be shown to learn to produce $V_{ij}(\infty) > \hat{V}$ in response to P_i if $c_{ij} > 0$ or to produce $V_{ij}(\infty) < \hat{V}$ if $c_{ij} < 0$, even if the buffer size is as small as $n = 1$ and the delay to reinforcement is $D > 1$.

Result   *The maximum delay over which learning is possible is independent of buffer size, but depends on the attention-setting function and on the decrement δ governing how attention decays with time.*

Argument   If pattern $P_i(t)$ generates output $a_j(t)$ and is assigned attention $att_{ij}(t) = f(\hat{V})$, it will be in the buffer D cycles later, and therefore be reinforced, if the following two conditions are satisfied.

$$f(\hat{V}) - (D - 1)\delta > 0 \qquad (5.6)$$

and

for all $t', t < t' < D$,
when input $P_k(t')$ appears,
and action $a_m(t')$ is output,

$$f(V_{km}(t')) < f(\hat{V}) - (t' - t)\delta \qquad (5.7)$$

Since $f(\hat{V}) = 1.0$ is a maximum, by Equation (5.3), the state including $P_i(t)$, $a_j(t)$ and their associated attention is guaranteed to at least enter the buffer when it first appears at time t – since the response it elicits will still be equal to $\hat{V}$. In order for it to receive its elicited reinforcement, it must still be in the buffer at time $t + D$, and Equations (5.6) and (5.7) describe the conditions ensuring this. Equation (5.6) requires simply that even though the attention to buffered P_i decreases by δ on each time step, the residual attention must still be non-zero at time $t + D$, $D - 1$ decrements after P_i enters the buffer at time t. Equation (5.7) requires that during this interval, no pattern P_k may elicit a response generating an attention which is higher than P_i's residual attention. These conditions would be satisfied if, for example, all patterns P_k appearing between times t and $t + D$ were very familiar and did not elicit high attentions. This might mean that P_i could not be learned until all intervening P_k had first been well learned, but eventually Equation (5.7) would then be satisfied.

As an example, given a system where $f(x) = \sin(\pi x / V_{MAX})$, $\delta = 0.1$, $V_{MAX} = 100$ and $\hat{V} = 50$, then by Equation (5.6), if $D < 11$, then P_i will receive at least one association with its own reinforcement. This limit on D could be increased if, for example, δ were decreased. Thus it is possible that, even with n as small as 1, indefinitely long delays may be bridged, depending on construction of f, δ, and $\hat{V}$.

This is not however the same as asserting that the system as a whole will necessarily learn the correct response to pattern P_i: namely, that $V_{ij}(\infty) \to V_{MAX}$ if $c_{ij} > 0$ or $V_{ij}(\infty) \to 0$ if $c_{ij} < 0$. In fact, this can only take place if D is further constrained.

Result   *The maximum delay over which the response to P_i will converge to 0 or to V_{MAX} depends on f, δ, and the reinforcement rates β^+ and β^-, but is still independent of n.*

Argument   Clearly, conditions (5.6) and (5.7) are still necessary, but an additional condition is needed. Consider the case when $c_{ij} > 0$ (the argument is symmetrical for $c_{ij} < 0$), and assume (the ideal case) that the system has already learned enough that for all patterns $P_k \neq P_i$, eliciting output a_m, $f(V_{km}(t)) = 0$. This ensures that (5.7) is satisfied, and P_i will be able to remain in the buffer until its reinforcement arrives. When this occurs, the response to P_i will be altered in such a way that each neural network within the learning system becomes more likely to output a vote for action a_j; overall, the sum of these votes V_{ij} will therefore rise. However, as V_{ij} rises, $att_{ij} = f(V_{ij})$ falls, by Equation (5.3), since $V_{ij} \geq \hat{V}$. After a critical number of reinforcements, V_{ij} will have risen so far that att_{ij} falls so far that it will have decayed to 0 before reinforcement c_{ij} arrives D time steps later. At this point, the response to P_i can no longer receive any further association with c_{ij}.

However, a minimum number m of reinforcements *must* be made to P_i, if P_i is to approach V_{MAX}.

In order for V_{ij} to approach V_{MAX}, it must be true that even after $m - 1$ reinforcements have been associated with P_i, att_{ij} is still high enough not to decay within D time steps.

In a single-layer PLN network, with $\Phi(x) = x$, a given pattern produces output $y_j = 1$ from node j with probability equal to $loc_j(t)[add_j]$. If a proportion $\hat{V}/V_{MAX}$ of the V_{MAX} nodes output 1, and if all nodes have been initialized to the same stored value $\hat{s}$, then it is consistent to assume that, on average,

$$\frac{V_{ij}(t)}{V_{MAX}} = \frac{\sum\limits_{j=1}^{V_{MAX}} loc_j(t)[add_j]}{V_{MAX}} \tag{5.8}$$

After one reinforcement β^r to node j

$$\Delta loc_j[add_j] = \Delta \Pr(y_j = 1) = \beta^r \tag{5.9}$$

by Equation (5.5). From Equation (5.9), and since $V_{MAX} = MAX$, after one reinforcement

$$\frac{V_{ij}(t+1)}{V_{MAX}} = \frac{\sum\limits_{j=1}^{V_{MAX}} (loc_j(t)[add_j]) + \beta^r}{V_{MAX}} = \frac{1}{V_{MAX}} \sum\limits_{j=1}^{V_{MAX}} (loc_j(t)[add_j]) + \beta^r \quad (5.10)$$

Substituting in Equation (5.8)

$$\frac{V_{ij}(t+1)}{V_{MAX}} = \frac{V_{ij}(t)}{V_{MAX}} + \beta^r \quad (5.11)$$

But, by definition, prior to any reinforcement, $V_{ij}(t) = \hat{V}$. So, after one reinforcement

$$\frac{V_{ij}(t+1)}{V_{MAX}} = \frac{\hat{V}}{V_{MAX}} \quad (5.12)$$

Therefore, after m reinforcement to P_i

$$\frac{V_{ij}(t+m)}{V_{MAX}} = \frac{\hat{V}}{V_{MAX}} + m\beta^r \quad (5.13)$$

Since m represents the number of reinforcements needed for V_{ij} to approach V_{MAX}

$$m \geqslant \frac{V_{MAX} - \hat{V}}{V_{MAX}\beta^r} \quad (5.14)$$

P_i must then generate sufficient attention att_{ij} after $m - 1$ reinforcements to generate still one more (after which $V_{ij} \geqslant V_{MAX}$)

$$f\left(\frac{\hat{V}}{V_{MAX}} + (m-1)\beta^r\right) - (D-1)\delta > 0 \quad (5.15)$$

This is the third condition which the system must satisfy for it to be possible that the response to pattern P_i converges to 1.

As an example, given the same system as above where $f(x) = \sin(\pi x / V_{MAX})$, $V_{MAX} = 100$, $\hat{V} = 50$, and $\delta = 0.1$, with $\beta^+ = 0.1$, then by Equation (5.14), $m \geqslant 5$, and so by Equation (5.15), $D \leqslant 4$.

It is possible to work out this maximum D explicitly, as well. Given the same system, at the time of the first reinforcement, $V_{ij}^0 = \hat{V} = 50$, and so $att_{ij} = f(V_{ij}^0) = 1.0$. At the time of the second reinforcement, $V_{ij}^1 = \hat{V} + V_{MAX}\beta^r = 60$, and so $att_{ij} = f(V_{ij}^1) = 0.95$. By the time of the fifth reinforcement to P_i, $V_{ij}^4 = \hat{V} + 4V_{MAX}\beta^r = 90$, and so $att_{ij} = f(V_{ij}^4) = 0.31$. This will be the last reinforcement available to P_i, since V_{ij} will then rise to V_{MAX}, and $f(V_{MAX}) = 0$. Therefore, the attention 0.31 must not decay to 0 within $D - 1$ time steps, so that pattern P_i paired with action a_j may still be in the buffer when that reinforcement arrives. But since $\delta = 0.1$, attention will decay to 0 within four time steps. Therefore, it is necessary to restrict $D \leqslant 4$. This matches the value derived above using Equations (5.14) and (5.15).

The conditions of Equations (5.6), (5.7) and (5.15) represent the minimum conditions under which learning and convergence to $V_{ij}(\infty) = 0$ or $V_{ij}(\infty) = V_{MAX}$ could take place. If learning about one pattern influences the response to another (as happens in updating a distributed memory) or if both positive and negative reinforcement occur (so that P_i could receive contradictory reinforcement during its stay in the buffer), the situation is more complicated, and the maximum D permissible under ideal conditions may not be workable in practice.

However, as the next sections in this chapter show, there are a series of heuristics which can guide in the construction of an ADB system and which maximize the probability that the given problem can be learned successfully.

5.2 Training set and learning rule

If both positive and negative reinforcements are liable to arrive, and so the reinforcement to $P_i \in M^+$ may be tempered by opposing reinforcements, P_i will be learned correctly if the average net reinforcement to each pattern $P_k \in M^-$ should be negative.

In general, if the buffer is of size n, and if $[1/\delta] < n$, most patterns will stay in the buffer for n time steps, particularly in the early stages of training, when all patterns generate the same response $\hat{V}$ and hence the same attention. Then it is to be expected that the rate of arrival of positive reinforcement during a pattern's stay is related to the proportion of positive patterns which exist: $|M^+|/|M|$. And if the pattern stays in the buffer long enough it will also receive the reinforcement which it itself elicited, c_{ij}. These expectations can be used to define the expected average net reinforcement which a pattern receives during a stay in the buffer. During a stay of n time steps, it should receive on average n reinforcements, which are positive with a probability related to the frequency with which positive patterns are encountered, and one of which will be the reinforcement it itself elicited.

Formally, the average net reinforcement $\overline{\Delta_{pos}}$ to $P_i \in M^+$ and $\overline{\Delta_{neg}}$ to $P_k \in M^-$ must satisfy

$$\overline{\Delta_{pos}} = \sum_{j=1}^{n-1} \left(\frac{|M^-|}{|M|} \beta^- + \frac{|M^+|}{|M|} \beta^+ \right) + \beta^+ > 0 \qquad (5.16)$$

$$\overline{\Delta_{neg}} = \sum_{j=1}^{n-1} \left(\frac{|M^-|}{|M|} \beta^- + \frac{|M^+|}{|M|} \beta^+ \right) + \beta^- < 0 \qquad (5.17)$$

In the example of section 4.2, $|M^+|/|M| = 10/11, |M^-|/|M| = 1/11$, and $n = 3$, giving the simultaneous equations

$$0 < (3-1)(\tfrac{1}{11}\beta^- + \tfrac{10}{11}\beta^+) + \beta^+ \qquad (5.18)$$

$$0 > (3-1)(\tfrac{1}{11}\beta^- + \tfrac{10}{11}\beta^+) + \beta^- \qquad (5.19)$$

These yield the inequality $1.5\beta^- < -\beta^- < 15.5\beta^+$; the values used in section 4.2, of $\beta^+ = 0.05$ and $\beta^- = -0.25$, satisfy this.

In the example of section 4.4, where $|M^+|/|M| = 23/26$, $|M^-|/|M| = 3/26$, and $n = 5$, the inequality derived is $2.4\beta^+ < -\beta^- < 9.8\beta^+$. Again, the values of $\beta^+ = 0.05$ and $\beta^- = -0.25$ satisfy this.

5.3 Learning system topology

The primary restriction on the topology of the learning system in an ADB system is that it be able to create output which is interpretable as a range, indicating strength of or confidence in a decision to act. This is most straight-forward when only two outputs are possible (e.g., accept or reject an input) and when the learning system is organized as a series of neural networks, each of which can contribute a vote as to the final action. In this case, the attention given to a decision to accept can be defined relative to the proportion of the number of networks outputting an accept vote. The example ADB systems discussed so far (in sections 4.2 and 4.4) have had a series of neural networks each collapsed to the level of a single PLN. Other topologies are possible, but this one is especially easy to analyze.

Given that the learning system consists of a series of PLNs, and that output $y_j = 1$ is defined as an accept vote from node j, the relevant parameters remaining are N, the number of PLNs; I, the number of inputs to each PLN (as opposed to the B bits composing the full input pattern), and ψ, the minimum number of PLNs which must output $y_j = 1$ in order for an accept output to be generated by the system. (If $\psi = V_{MAX}/2$, the system simply outputs according to majority vote.) These three parameters interact in such a way as to determine the learnability of both the positive and negative patterns within the training set – irrespective of delay D or buffer size n.

To learn a given problem, no more than $\psi - 1$ PLNs may output 1 in response to any $P_k \in M^-$, while at least ψ must output 1 in response to each $P_i \in M^+$. Because PLNs are being used, this translates into the restriction that each P_k will address a location in each PLN, and at least $N - \psi + 1$ of these locations must not also be addressed by any P_i; simultaneously, each P_i addresses a location in each PLN, and in at least ψ of the PLNs these must be locations not addressed by any P_k. These criteria are stricter than they would need to be if the learning system contained multi-layer networks. So, the problem is to ensure that enough nodes have locations which are not addressed by elements of M^- and both M^+.

First, considering one $P_k \in M^-$ and one PLN j, the probability $\Lambda^-(P_k)$ that

P_k addresses the same location in j as at least one positive pattern is given as

$$\Lambda^-(P_k) = \sum_{x=1}^{|M^+|} (-1)^{x+1} \mathbf{Pr}(x, P_k, M^+) \tag{5.20}$$

$\mathbf{Pr}(x, P_k, M^+)$ is defined as the probability that a random I bits of the input pattern are chosen as the input to node j which are identical in exactly x patterns of M^+; that is also the probability that a random node j receives all of its inputs from bits which are identical in exactly x patterns in M^+. This is given by Aleksander and Wilson's formula (1985) – see also Equations 3.24 and 3.25 – and may also be expressed as

$$\mathbf{Pr}(x, P_k, M^+) = \sum_{\bar{v}_{y;M^+}} A(\bar{v}_{y,M^+}, P_k) \tag{5.21}$$

where $\bar{v}_{y,M^+}$ is a set of y patterns selected from M^+, and $A(\bar{v}_{y,M^+}, P_k)$ is the overlap between P_k and these y patterns.

Given the probability $\Lambda^-(P_k)$ that an overlap occurs in one node, the probability that overlap occurs in at most $\psi - 1$ nodes, and hence that pattern P_k is learnable, is

$$\Pr(P_k \text{ learnable}) = \sum_{w=0}^{\psi-1} \binom{N}{w} \Lambda^-(P_k)^w (1 - \Lambda^-(P_k))^{N-w} \tag{5.22}$$

and the probability P_{neg} that all negative patterns $P_k \in M^-$ are learnable is

$$P_{neg} = \Pr(M^- \text{ learnable}) = \prod_{P_k \in M^-} \sum_{w=0}^{\psi-1} \binom{N}{w} \Lambda^-(P_k)^w (1 - \Lambda^-(P_k))^{N-w} \tag{5.23}$$

The probability that a single $P_i \in M^+$ is learnable can be derived in exactly the same way. First, the probability $\Lambda^+(P_i)$ that P_i addresses the same location in a node j as at least one negative pattern is

$$\Lambda^+(P_i) = \sum_{x=1}^{M^-} (-1)^{x+1} \mathbf{Pr}(x, P_i, M^-) \tag{5.24}$$

The probability that this does not occur is $1 - \Lambda^+(P_i)$. The probability that there is no such overlap between P_i and any element of M^- for at least ψ nodes, and hence that P_i is learnable, is therefore

$$\Pr(P_i \text{ learnable}) = \sum_{m=\psi}^{N} \binom{N}{w} (1 - \Lambda^+(P_i))^w \Lambda^+(P_i)^{N-w} \tag{5.25}$$

Finally, the probability P_{pos} that all $P_i \in M^+$ are learnable is

$$P_{pos} = \Pr(M^+ \text{ learnable}) = \prod_{P_i \in M^+} \sum_{w=\psi}^{N} \binom{N}{w} (1 - \Lambda^+(P_i))^w \Lambda^+(P_i)^{N-\omega} \tag{5.26}$$

To learn all of $M = M^+ \cup M^-$, the parameters ψ, N, and I should be constructed so that both P_{neg} and P_{pos} are maximized.

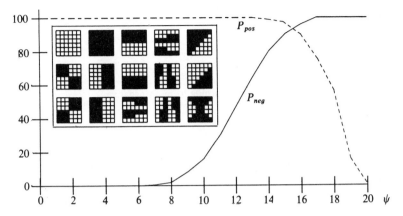

Figure 5.1 *Influence of ψ on* P_{neg} *and* P_{pos}, *inset shows* M *used.* M^- *consists of the left-most column,* M^+ *contains the remaining 12 patterns.*

For a given M, **Pr**( ) decreases as I increases, and so both P_{neg} and P_{pos} also increase. However, as I increases to a PLN, the storage requirements of the network also increase exponentially, while the generalization abilities begin to be restricted, as explained in Chapter 3. If $I = B$, at the extreme, the node is simply a look-up table recording the correct output for each complete input pattern, without the capability for any generalization at all. For these reasons, it is usually neither practical nor desirable to set I very high.

On the other hand, as ψ increases, P_{neg} increases while P_{pos} decreases. For example, for the training set shown in Figure 4.2, and using a learning system containing $N = 20$ PLNs each with $I = 4$ inputs, the resulting values of P_{pos} and P_{neg} are as shown in Figure 5.1.

The curves of Figure 5.1 predict that the ability to learn to reject all negative patterns should steadily increase with ψ, reaching expected perfect performance by about $\psi \approx 17$, while with $\psi \geqslant 16$, the value of P_{pos} falls and the ability to reliably accept all negative patterns should be impaired.

In fact, in computer simulations, this is exactly •what occurs. Figure 5.2 shows that systems display improving ability to learn to reject all negative patterns as ψ grows, while as ψ passes 17, the systems begin also to reject positive patterns. The number of negative reinforcements, a measure of learning time, is high for low ψ, as the system *never* learns to reject the negative patterns; learning time is low and fairly constant for $14 \leqslant \psi \leqslant 17$, in which range most nets learn to reject the negative and accept all the positive patterns. For $\psi > 17$, learning time increases: as there are fewer ways to distribute the necessary ψ accept votes among N nodes as ψ rises.

For systems where there is a large mass of training data or many nodes within the learning system, the equations defining P_{neg} and P_{pos} may not be trivial to solve, even with the aid of a computer. However, an exact solution

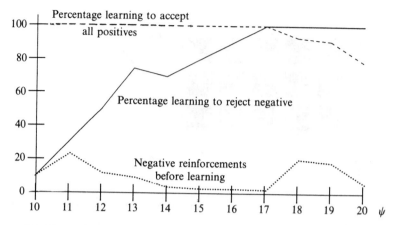

Figure 5.2 *Observed acceptance rates of positive and negative patterns as a function of ψ. M taken from Figure 4.2; each point represents average of 20 experiments.*

is probably not necessary in the general case. It may suffice to understand how the parameter ψ affects P_{neg} (directly) and P_{pos} (inversely). During training on a given problem, if the system seems unable to learn to reject all negative patterns, then ψ should be raised; if the system does not consistently accept all positive patterns, ψ is too high and should be lowered. Finally, it is quite possible that there is no value of ψ for a given N, I and M for which both P_{neg} and P_{pos} will approach 1. In this situation, a good choice of ψ depends on whether it is more acceptable to suffer false rejections of positive patterns or false acceptances of negative ones.

5.4 Construction of nodes

A last major class of parameter to be considered defines the nodes within the learning system. For a network of PLNs, the parameters are the number of inputs I, the learning rates β^+ and β^-, the output probability function Φ^P, and the initial stored value $\hat{s}$. The first three were discussed in a previous section and so their choice is already constrained.

The output probability function Φ^P describes the probability that $\Phi(x) = 1$, for a given x. Several possible Φ^P were discussed in Chapter 3; for example the 'soft' output function

$$\Phi_s^P(x) = \Pr(j \text{ outputs } 1 \,|\, x = loc_j[add_j]) = x \qquad (5.27)$$

and the 'hard' output function

$$\Phi_H^P(x) = \Pr(j \text{ outputs } 1 \,|\, x = loc_j[add_j]) = 0 \qquad \text{if } x < 0.5$$
$$= 1 \qquad \text{if } x > 0.5$$
$$= 0.5 \qquad \text{if } x = 0.5 \qquad (5.28)$$

The soft function allows for a degree of randomness in transformation from addressed value to output, while the hard function ensures that as soon as the addressed value has been incremented away even once from $\hat{s}$, the output will reliably reflect the direction in which learning is proceeding.

Both types of output function – and the infinite number of sigmoidal functions intermediate between the two – are useful in various circumstances. For example, a soft output function is most desirable when the learning system should be very exploratory, and not commit itself easily to outputting a single value under a particular input. The hard output function, on the other hand, usually leads to fastest convergence of the network to stable unchanging outputs in response to each input pattern (Myers, 1989).

In the case of an ADB system using a hard output function, if a (positive) pattern appears close in time with a negative pattern, there is a risk that after a single association of that pattern with the negative reinforcement, the hard output function will ensure that that pattern is never again accepted. Use of a soft output function increases the possibility that a pattern which has received negative reinforcement once or twice, perhaps because it appears close in time to a negative pattern, will still occasionally be accepted. In this way it is possible for the system to 'recover' that pattern: if these occasional accepts are positively reinforced, and the negative pattern is no longer being accepted, the system can learn that the pattern is positive.

For this reason, the output functions used in most of the ADB simulations which are discussed in this book use $\Phi^P = \Phi_s^P$ as in Equation (5.27) – the soft output function.

A final parameter defining the PLN is $\hat{s}$, the value to which all locations in all nodes j are initialized. The probability that an untrained node will output $y_j = 1$ in response to a random input is $\Phi^P(\hat{s})$. $\hat{s}$ therefore determines the system's initial predisposition to accept patterns

$$\Pr(accept) = \sum_{w=\psi}^{N} \binom{N}{w} \hat{s}^w (1 - \hat{s})^{N-w} \tag{5.29}$$

Given $N = 20$ and $\psi = 17$ from the previous example, the probability that a random pattern will be accepted, according to this equation, is as shown in Figure 5.3. Since it was determined above that ψ should be set at or near 17, Figure 5.3 shows that if $\hat{s}$ were set to 0.5, it would be unlikely that the system would ever accept a pattern. Since the ADB systems are exploratory, and all reinforcements come as the result of actions, any system which never acts cannot learn anything. It is therefore vital that $\hat{s}$ be chosen so that at least in the beginning the system has a high predisposition to accept patterns.

If the output probability function Φ^P is a hard function, the situation is even more dramatic: for $\hat{s} < 0.5$, the output of each node y_j is constrained to be 0. In this case no accept actions will ever occur! It is therefore vital that $\hat{s} \geqslant 0.5$.

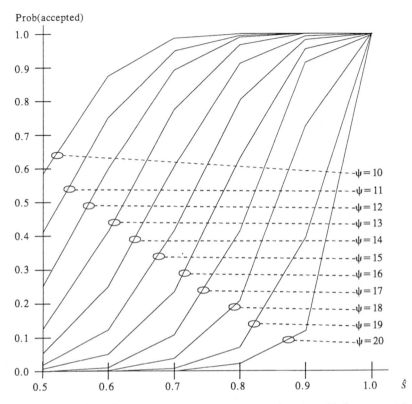

Figure 5.3 *Probability of accepting a random pattern as a function of ŝ, for a net with*
N = 20, at various ψ.

However, using a high $\hat{s}$ means that more negative reinforcements will be
required before the system learns to stop accepting a negatively reinforced
pattern. After one negative reinforcement to a stored value $loc_j[add_j]$, in the
average case

$$\Delta loc_j[add_j] = \overline{\Delta_{neg}} \qquad (5.30)$$

where $\overline{\Delta_{neg}}$ is the average net reinforcement to a negative pattern as defined
in section 5.1. Then, after m such reinforcements, $loc_j[add_j]$ will be equal to
$\hat{s} + m\overline{\Delta_{neg}}$. The system will have fully learned to reject the pattern when
$loc_j[add_j] < 0.0$, and therefore when

$$\hat{s} + m\overline{\Delta_{neg}} \leqslant 0.0$$

$$m \geqslant \frac{\hat{s}}{\overline{\Delta_{neg}}} \qquad (5.31)$$

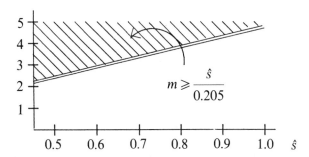

Figure 5.4 *The relationship between m (minimum accepts of negative pattern required before learning) and ŝ. Shaded area satisfies Equations (4.32).*

In the example computed in section 5.2, where $|M^+|/|M| = 10/11$, $|M^-|/|M| = 1/11, n = 3, \beta^+ = 0.05$ and $\beta^- = -0.25$, this yields the expression

$$m \geqslant \frac{\hat{s}}{0.205} \tag{5.32}$$

This relation is shown graphically in Figure 5.4. It shows that there is a linear increase with $\hat{s}$ in the number of accepts needed before the system learns not to accept a negative pattern. In general, each negative pattern appears with frequency $1/|M|$, and so the total number m_{tot} of accepts needed before the system will have learned the problem scales as

$$m_{tot} = m|M| \geqslant \frac{\hat{s}|M|}{0.205} \tag{5.33}$$

In practice, a value of $\hat{s}$ is required which compromises between the drive to increase it (to insure accepts occur at all) and to decrease it (tending to reduce the time to learn to stop accepting negative patterns).

5.5 Generalization tests

One important aspect of neural network learning has not been addressed so far in the analysis of ADB systems: generalization. Generalization may be defined as the ability of a system, when presented with a novel pattern, to respond to it in the same way as it does to the trained pattern nearest to it. Nearness is often taken to refer to Hamming distance between pattern. Other distance metrics may be used, but Hamming distance is usually relevant for pattern recognition problems.

The provision of a buffer, attention-setting mechanism and so on are useful only during training, allowing the system to cope with delayed reinforcement. Once the problem has been learned successfully, if the environment is not subject to change, only the neural network learning system is still relevant.

At this point, the full ADB system could be replaced by the neural network alone, as long as no further delay learning is required.

For this reason, the ADB neural network is capable of precisely the same generalization as an identical topology *not* embedded within an ADB system, and any existing analysis of its capabilities applies.

It has been stressed in Chapter 3 that networks of PLNs do not generalize at the node level but at the network level. Since each node in a single-layer network sees only a fraction of the total external input, it can only base its response on that portion of the input which it sees. This means that the node will respond in the same way to all external input patterns which share at least those I bits. In general, since there are 2^B possible B-bit input patterns, but only 2^I possible input combinations to an I-input node, each node will generalize its response to novel patterns by responding in the same way as it does to trained patterns which contain the same I-bit address. This translates into generalization at the network level, as each node outputs a response to the novel pattern identical to that for the trained patterns which provide the same input to that node.

As an example of generalization in action by an ADB system, a task can be set involving training on the 26 36-bit letter patterns used as input to the bug system (shown in Figure 4.7), and then tested with increasingly distorted versions of those patterns. Ideally, the system should be able to generalize and respond to these novel patterns in the same way as it responds to the trained patterns from which they are derived. Patterns A, B, ... F were defined as negative, patterns G, H, ... Z were positive, and all reinforcements arrived with delay $D = 5$.

The system used in this task contained $N = 25$, 10-input PLNs, with $\hat{s} = 1.00$ and $\Phi^P(x) = x$. The system output an accept decision if at least $\psi = 23$ nodes output $y_j = 1$, and maintained a buffer of size $n = 5$. Nodes were updated by $\beta^+ = 0.05$ and $\beta^- = -0.25$; attention was set as shown in Figure 4.3 and decayed by $\delta = 0.1$ with each time step spent in the buffer. These parameters were derived from the constraints imposed by the training set and the heuristics developed in this chapter.

The system was first trained to respond correctly to all 26 training patterns, which it did within about 21,000 training steps or about 800 passes through the complete training set. The task is not trivial, as there is high overlap between elements of M^+ and M^- – for instance between patterns G and C (89% bits the same) or between patterns O and A (81% bits the same). (In fact, of 20 nets trained on this task, 10% failed to learn to reject all six negative patterns within 50,000 training steps.)

Once the system was trained perfectly, it was tested with novel, distorted versions of the training patterns. The distortion consisted of a random inversion of some percentage of bits in the pattern. The system was said to have generalized successfully if it output the same response as to the original undistorted version of the pattern. Figure 5.5 shows that the system

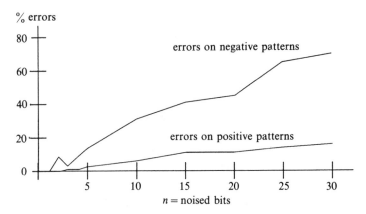

Figure 5.5 *Average generalization to disrupted versions of positive and negative patterns, taken from a single ADB system, during ten presentation of each of the 20 positive and 6 negative training patterns.*

generalized quite successfully for low rates of distortion, and performance then degraded in an approximately linear fashion as the rate of distortion grew.

There are two particularly relevant points to note about Figure 5.5. First, the performance degrades in a relatively slow fashion; for distortion of less than 5 in 64 bits (or up to 12.5% noise), the number of patterns eliciting incorrect responses stays below 10%. Second, the error rate for positive patterns increases more slowly than that for negative patterns. One likely cause of this is simply that since $|M^+| > |M^-|$, the trained net is biased to output accept decisions; if a novel pattern is closer in Hamming distance to some unrelated training pattern P_i than to the training pattern P_k from which it was actually derived, the odds are that $P_i \in M^+$, and that the system will respond with an accept decision, thereby outputting the 'correct' decision if $P_k \in M^+$ but 'incorrect' if $P_k \in M^-$.

5.6 Attention-driven buffering: conclusions

The major heuristics derived in this chapter can be restated as follows.

- The choice of buffer size n does not necessarily limit the maximum delay D over which the ADB system can still learn – even if $n = 1$; instead, the system is more likely to be able to associate a reinforcement with an input–output pair which occurred D time steps previously if $f(\hat{V})$ (the attention to a novel pattern) is high and δ (the amount by which attention decays with each time step) is low. Figure 4.5 showed that increased n does tend to result in learning and an increased *likelihood* that patterns will be associated with appropriate reinforcement, but the point is that such learning is still possible even with n much smaller than D.

- The reinforcement rates β^+ and β^- by which the neural networks are updated during training must be chosen dependent on the expected proportion of positive and negative patterns within the training set. In particular, if the proportion of positive patterns is significantly larger, then β^- should be chosen significantly larger than β^+, and vice versa. This is because if a state remains in the buffer for a number of time steps, it is liable to be associated with incoming reinforcement at each of those time steps; its own reinforcement must be large enough to, on average, counteract the net reinforcement it receives from spurious sources.

- Consider a system where a certain number ψ of neural networks must output a vote to 'accept' if such action is to be taken by the system, and where otherwise the system output is to 'reject' the current input pattern. Then as ψ rises, it becomes harder to accept any pattern, and so it is more likely that the system can learn to reject all negative patterns within the training set. Simultaneously, as ψ rises, it also becomes harder to accept positive training patterns, and so there is an increasing probability that the system will also learn not to accept one or more positive patterns. An optimal intermediate value of ψ maximizes the probability of learning to reject all negative patterns while minimizing the probability that positive patterns are rejected.

- If the learning system is based on PLN networks, the choice of $\hat{s}$ to which all stored values in all nodes are initialized determines the initial propensity of the system to act in response to random input. Because the ADB system is exploratory, it only receives reinforcement in response to actions, and therefore, if the system does not have an initial high predisposition to act, it will never learn anything. This implies that $\hat{s}$ should be set high, on the assumption that this will lead to more nodes voting for action (e.g., accept) in response to random input patterns. However, as $\hat{s}$ grows, it will take longer to train each node *not* to accept negative patterns, and therefore training time increases.

- It is to be expected that generalization capability of a trained ADB system will be identical to that of a trained learning system of the same topology but trained without delayed results (e.g., by mapping the problem to be learned onto a simple pattern association task). Therefore, any knowledge about topologies useful within a problem domain can be applied to solving instances of the problem which involve delayed learning and therefore indicate an ADB system should be used.

The attention-setting function f has so far been considered either as a sine curve, or else as a plateaued step function, if this simplification does not seem costly in terms of system performance. The overall shape is clearly required to yield low or zero values for low and high vote tallies, and maximal values for intermediate vote tallies, but there is a wide range of curves which satisfy these criteria. Yet the exact choice of maxima and minima as well as the shape of f remain essentially arbitrary.

One extension which would be interesting to consider is the possibility of an f which changes with time. Instead of being a fixed function, the attention could be generated by a module which is itself adaptive, and which maps from a vote tally to a scalar output. Another interesting extension would be to use an f which considered other aspects beyond the simple vote tally generated by an input. Such a function might, for example, consider the overall goal of the system: if the current goal is to find shelter, this might lower the attention to inputs associated with finding food, however novel they might be.

A second aspect of the standard ADB paradigm which could be made sophisticated is the decay rate for attention of states in the buffer. Instead of being a constant $0 \leqslant \delta \leqslant 1$, the attention could decay as a function not merely of the previous value, but also of external parameters. For example, attention could be re-inflated by a phenomenon similar in effect to rehearsal in human short-term memory. Human short-term memory is widely defined as a buffer which can store a finite number of items for a few seconds (Eysenck, 1984); the capacity was famously quantified by Miller (1956) as 'seven plus or minus two' items, but these items can apparently range in complexity from simple letters to complex words or concepts. Material in short-term memory can be maintained as long as it is being processed: a familiar form of processing is rehearsal, which often involves repeating the material aloud or under the breath. Another external parameter usefully affecting attention would be the recognition that some input–output pair (although perhaps usually eliciting perfectly predictable reinforcement) was going to be important this time – and therefore should be assigned a high attention to ensure it a lengthy stay in the buffer.

The ADB system could achieve these effects if it were provided with capabilities for assigning attention based on other factors in addition to novelty or unpredictability. It could either initialize the attention of 'important' states to an inflated level, thereby lengthening the maximum duration of their stay in the buffer, or else repeatedly refresh attention by supplying periodic increments to the attention of 'important' buffered states. The decision of which states are 'important' would seem to imply the existence of a higher-level controller, which determines current goals and possibly current plans for achieving those goals. This controller could then recognize that some events are relevant to these goals and plans, and dictate inflated original attention or repeated refreshment of attention as appropriate.

6

An ADB system for operant conditioning

One of the primary reasons why learning under conditions of delayed reinforcement is important is that it is such an integral part of animal learning. The last chapter mentioned the relation of operant conditioning to delay learning: in operant conditioning, there is always at least a slight delay between action taken and the receipt of reward. Even if this delay lasts only for a few milliseconds, that is already several 'time steps' in the language of the neural firing rates of the brain.

It may seem then that the solution to this problem of delay learning in operant conditioning would simply be to 'freeze' the states of the neurons which are responsible for processing the stimulus representation – so that the representation is held intact and available until reinforcement arrives. There are several inadequacies with this approach: the simplest being that in some cases no reinforcement arrives, and so the system would hold an image indefinitely at great physical cost. Worse, if the stimulus is for example a visual image, the animal will be unable to process any new visual stimuli while it awaits reinforcement, because the necessary neurons are frozen!

A better approach is to buffer the stimulus representations in such a way that they do not interfere with the ongoing processing of stimuli by the system. This may be done by copying the representations into a buffer somewhere else, where the representation can be maintained somehow until reinforcement arrives and it is recovered. Alternatively the representation can be stored in the same neurons (or brain regions) responsible for processing it, as long as the storage mechanisms are separate from and do not interfere with the ongoing processing of stimuli by these neurons. Functionally, these two approaches may be much the same, and either is preferable to the freezing of neurons needed for that ongoing processing.

ADB represents one suggestion of how a buffering strategy can be implemented. In ADB, stimulus representations are stored (either in the processing cells or somewhere else) until reinforcement arrives, but do not interfere with the system's processing of subsequent stimuli.

As it turns out, a system using ADB in this way can learn to solve problems which are parallel to operant conditioning tasks to which animals can be trained: one objective which led to the development of ADB. This chapter describes a series of experiments which are meant to be comparable to existing experiments with one particular animal: the common octopus.

The octopus is one of the 'simplest' animals which is still capable of sophisticated learning of the type required, and it has been extensively studied, so that there is a large body of data (derived largely from the pioneering work of Young, Wells, Boycott and their colleagues) with which the results from ADB simulations can be compared. But these experiments are primarily interesting as indications of how an ADB system compares with an example of one animal performing a class of operant conditioning task. There is another sense in which the system can be compared to the octopus *per se*, in that the architecture of its learning systems is similar and in that it degrades in similar ways after various kinds of damage, but that discussion is delayed until the next chapter.

This chapter instead concentrates on the performance of an ADB system at a task which is derived from a typical operant conditioning task within the animal learning paradigm.

6.1 The operant conditioning task

An operant conditioning task has already been defined as one in which the animal receives a particular non-specific reinforcement contingent on a particular response. This is a delay learning task in a temporal sense, since there is always a slight delay between response and reinforcement (and even until the reinforcement is recognized by central learning areas). It is also the case that there is intervening information during this delay.

The type of visual discrimination task usually presented to the octopus in a laboratory set-up involves the presentation of one or more geometric shapes or objects presented visually or tactilely and each assigned a reinforcement value. If the animal reaches for and grasps a positive object it will obtain the positive reinforcement (usually a bit of food); if it does not grasp or even pushes away a negative object, it will avoid the negative reinforcement (usually a mild but aversive electric shock). This type of task can be decomposed into a series of distinct stages:

1. the presentation of the stimulus;
2. the decision to accept (approach and grasp) or reject (retreat from or simply fail to accept);
3. the approach or retreat;
4. the grasping of an accepted stimulus;
5. the drawing under the mantle of an accepted stimulus; and
6. the receipt of positively reinforcing taste or negatively reinforcing shock.

Not all stages occur on every trial, and the stages are not necessarily discrete. For example, the octopus may approach the object but then retreat without touching it, or reach out an arm without actually grasping the object. But at least in some cases, all six stages occur. When this happens, in addition to the time delay between the decision at stage 2 and the receipt of reinforcement at stage 6, the octopus first sees the distal stimulus, then sees a progressively larger retinal image as the object is approached, then a series of images in which the arm is superimposed over the object and the object is drawn in, and finally a series of images in which the object is not even visible as it is drawn under the mantle and into the mouth. All of these images are temporally closer to the reinforcement than the original stimulus image, and therefore if the octopus employed a delay reinforcement learning system based on contiguity of inputs (as do temporal difference methods, for example), then it would learn a great deal about associating visions of its own arm with food and much less about how to respond to stimuli at a distance. However, the octopus clearly *can* learn to make correct decisions about stimuli viewed distally: it does not need to draw objects in and examine them at close range before it can determine their expected reinforcement value. In fact, an animal which only had that ability to recognize prey and predators would not last very long in the wild.

Therefore, the octopus, and all animals which show the same kind of abilities, must at the very minimum have a mechanism for relating reinforcements with previous sensory stimuli: in particular, it should be able to assign reinforcement selectively to those sensory stimuli which are relevant, and ignore stimuli which appear prior to the conditioned stimulus, or which intervene between the original stimulus image and the receipt of reinforcement. This, of course, is addressed by ADB.

So, the first issue is to design a task for ADB systems which retains the important characteristics of the operant conditioning tasks learnable by an animal.

The most important short-coming of a task implementable on a digital computer is the necessary discretization of time. The visual system operates in continuous time: receptors and neurons output time-averaged frequency signals, and operate asynchronously. Simulated ANNs, on the other hand, generally operate in cycles and time steps: within one time step, each node is examined once and can update but then remains constant until the next time step.

This makes the problem of buffering images considerably easier in a network: since there are only a finite number of discrete stimulus patterns within any task, there can be a decision how to respond to each individually and whether each should be buffered. In continuous time, in the real world in which the animal must function, images are not discrete. However, a great deal of the visual system seems to be devoted to detecting *changes* (rather than magnitudes) in inputs. Therefore, perhaps it is still sensible to talk about particular images in the visual system, with the caveat that one image may be a time-averaged representation of activity over a series of receptors whose patterns of activity have remained relatively constant for a time.

The inputs to the ADB system (named OVSIM after 'Octopus vulgaris simulation') are binary images – again a concession to simulation; there is no reason in principle why the images could not be grey- level or coloured, but it does not add a new complexity to the problem. Some example input patterns are shown in Figure 6.1; since some octopus experiments involve the showing of one object and some of two, the stimulus patterns allow for one or two 'objects' to be present.

In the laboratory tank, the octopuses are provided with a 'home', usually consisting of a hollow inside a few bricks, and they usually remain within this home, as they would in the wild. They leave the home to jet out and capture food, and then return. Since the experimenters generally take care to present stimulus objects at a constant distance near the far end of the tank (Boycott and Young, 1955), it seems reasonable to assume that input images of the same object are equivalent, and this lends credence to the idea of using fixed patterns to represent retinal images of stimuli.

Both the octopus eye (like most animal eyes) and the OVSIM input system code visual stimuli in terms of such features as edges and brightness, and also in terms of perceived motion. For this reason, when a stimulus object is lowered into the tank, if the octopus does not respond immediately, the experimenter jiggles the object slightly at a constant rate, ensuring that

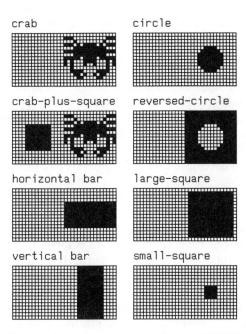

Figure 6.1 *The set of stimulus patterns used in the OVSIM simulations.*

motion-detecting receptors in the octopus eye continue to be stimulated. Usually, there is a maximum time such as two minutes for each trial (Boycott and Young, 1955), although other experiments involve differing trial lengths. If the animal does not respond within that time, the object is removed, and the trial is scored as a no-attack. In the same way, a stimulus pattern is presented to OVSIM for a maximum of, for example, 20 cycles, where one **cycle** is the processing time for OVSIM to operate upon a stimulus pattern and produce one output decision to attack or not. The pattern is jiggled up and down one bit after each cycle in which OVSIM does not output an attack decision, so that movement-detectors are stimulated. Each **trial** in an OVSIM experiment consists of a series of cycles of presentation of a single stimulus pattern, and terminates when an attack output is generated or when a maximum number of cycles (usually 20) have passed without attack to the pattern. If an attack occurs, a standard sequence of images of an arm superimposed over the pattern and drawing it down out of sight begins. This loosely represents the distortion which occurs between the decision to attack an object and the receipt of reinforcement. Reinforcement is signalled to OVSIM only at the end of this sequence. Figure 6.2 shows two example sequences in which attack outputs are generated.

This highlights another important difference between learning in a real animal and learning in OVSIM: OVSIM assumes that the decision to attack an object is indivisible and irreversible. That is, OVSIM cannot generate an attack output and then, after one or two cycles of approaching the stimulus, decide to reverse that decision. It is also the case that in OVSIM, re-inforcement always arrives at a constant number of cycles after the attack decision is output. Clearly, in the animal, negative reinforcement is delivered as soon as the animal touches the negative object, while positive reinforcement is postponed until ingestion. The situation in OVSIM is as if negative reinforcement would be delayed as well until the animal places the object into its mouth. This is perhaps more like the situation in the wild, where objects are more likely to be inedible than electrified.

Several other simplifications in the model are worth mentioning. First, in many animals with developed eyes, including octopus, there is some degree of binocularity – giving rise to redundant information, and even some information about depth. OVSIM contains only a single 'visual' system. It is as if the animal had been blinded in one eye: which does not have detrimental effect on learning. Next, in any animal, there are numerous systems operating in parallel with the one being conditioned. In octopus, for example, there are the influences of brain systems controlling diurnal behaviour fluctuations, skin patterning, mating, etc. All of these are ignored in OVSIM, as are the effects of a hunger system. Hunger, at least, is carefully controlled for in octopus experiments: the animals are maintained in a constant state of hunger (Young, 1960), to increase the reward value of the positive reinforcement, and it has been observed that once trained, the probability of the animal attacking an

BASIC SEQUENCE   POSITIVE SEQUENCE   NEGATIVE SEQUENCE

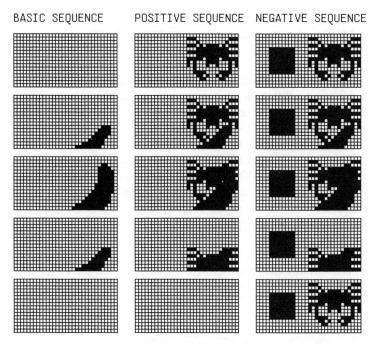

Figure 6.2 *Left: the patterns imposed over the input pattern during the five cycles of an accept sequence. Centre: the resulting augmented input to OVSIM during an accept sequence generated to a positive crab stimulus pattern; reinforcement arrives when the final (blank) pattern is current input. Right: the resulting augmented input during accept sequence to a negative crab-plus-square stimulus pattern; reinforcement arrives when the final (released) pattern is current.*

object is unrelated to its hunger (Young, 1958b). So this, at least, seems reasonable not to feature in the model.

Finally, OVSIM as implemented has no size generalization capability. In human beings, for example, learning about an object at one distance, and hence one retinal size, transfers when that object is presented at a different distance and different retinal size: adult humans can generalize and recognize the object when presented differently. However, octopuses have not been found to exhibit any significant generalization over size (Young, 1964); further, as mentioned above, the experimenter usually takes care to present the stimuli at a constant distance from the 'home' in which the octopus is to be found, thus ensuring a constant retinal size during trials.

6.2 Description of the simulation

The operant conditioning system, OVSIM (Myers 1991b), consists of two components. In the first, the binary 'raw' input patterns are re-coded by feature detectors into a basic description of their contents. In the second, an ADB system handles the association of these feature-based patterns with the eventual reinforcement. A schematic diagram of OVSIM appears in Figure 6.3.

The idea of a visual learning system containing as its first layer a set of feature-detecting cells is an ubiquitous one in higher visual systems. The pioneering work of Hubel and Wiesel provided evidence of edge-detecting neurons in cat (Hubel and Wiesel, 1965) and monkey (Hubel and Wiesel, 1968) visual cortex, while other seminal research revealed feature detectors in the early visual system of frog (Lettvin *et al.*, 1965), pigeon (Maturana and Frenk, 1963) and other animals. Whereas vertebrates have 5–6 layers of processing cells within the retina, the octopus retina contains only receptor cells. These send axons directly, via the crossed optic nerves, to the contralateral optic lobe, believed to be the seat of visual memory in octopus. It is here that feature detection is likely to begin.

While there is no clear consensus on exactly what features the octopus visual system preferentially encodes, there are a great deal of clues. Given that some discriminations are more easily learnable by the animal than others, some

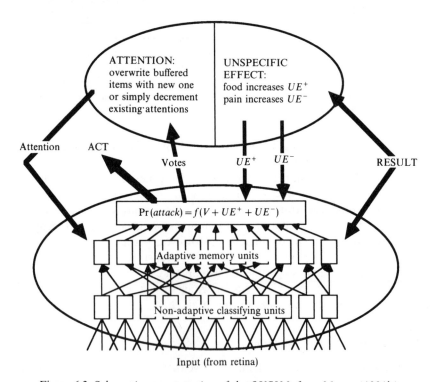

Figure 6.3 *Schematic representation of the OVSIM, from Myers (1991b).*

features may have special detectors within the retina. For example, the octopus more easily learns to discriminate horizontal from diagonal or vertical from diagonal than diagonal from diagonal (even though in the first two cases, the classes differ only by 45 degrees, while in the latter class, there are 90 degrees separating examples) (Sutherland, 1957). It is therefore likely that horizontal-ness and verticality are specially encoded by feature detectors.

However, the best way to uncover feature detectors is by single cell recording, which can demonstrate exactly which features activate a single neuron. In the absence of such experimentation with octopus *per se*, it is still the case that there are certain features which trigger the visual system in most species. Blakemore (1975) lists these as contrast, presence of edges, orientation of edges, presence of movement, direction of movement, convexity or size, and illumination or brightness.

The feature-encoding level of OVSIM was built along these general principles. The units in this level have 'receptive fields' which cover 3×3-bit regions of the raw input pattern, scanning the field for a particular feature, and outputting 1 if the feature is present in the current cycle and 0 otherwise. Since the input pattern measures 32×16 bits, there are 420 3×3-bit receptive fields which cover it.

Ten types of feature-encoding units exist. The 'whiteness' detectors fire if at least 8/9 of the bits in the receptive field are equal to 0; while the 'blackness' detectors fire if at least 8/9 are 1. The 'vertical edge' detectors fire if the receptive field contains perfect versions of vertical edges, the 'horizontal edge' detectors fire in a complementary way when horizontal edges occur. There are 'left', 'right', 'up' and 'down' movement detectors, which fire when an edge which was present in the last cycle's input has moved within the receptive field in the appropriate direction. Finally, 'on-centre' detectors fire when the centre bit in the receptive field is 1 but most of the surrounding bits within the field are 0, while 'off-centre' detectors compute the complementary function. Figure 6.4 shows the classes recognized by these feature detectors.

Each feature-detecting unit is implemented as a look-up table, storing the patterns to which it should output 1, and outputting 0 when the current pattern of bits within the receptive field matches none of these stored prototypes. One of each sort of unit monitors each of the receptive fields, so the output of this level is a recoding of the input pattern into a set of 4200 bits, encoding the presence and location of various kinds of features in the inputs.

It is worth emphasizing that the feature-detecting units, as implemented, are non-adapting; the response of a unit to any input is pre-determined. This has a parallel in the early sensory cortices of mammals, for example. Feature-detecting neurons there self-organize during a critical or sensitive period in infancy; during this period if, say, the environment consists uniformly of vertical bars, the animal will develop large numbers of cells which recognize verticality, and few which recognize horizontal edges. But after the critical period, this kind of reorganization does not occur, and the functions of feature-

Black   **White**

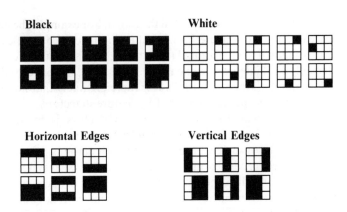

Horizontal Edges   **Vertical Edges**

Right Movement   **Left Movement**

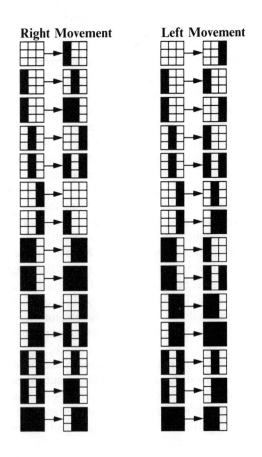

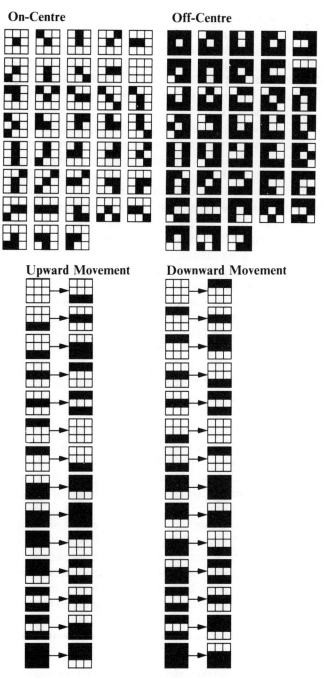

Figure 6.4 *The set of 3 × 3 retinal field inputs recognized by each class of feature-detecting unit in OVSIM, from Myers (1991b).*

detecting neurons remain relatively fixed (Blakemore, 1988)[1]. This seems logical; higher levels must learn discriminations and associations based on the feature encodings output by earlier levels. If the output of these early levels is subject to frequent and dramatic change, the information stored in higher levels will be quickly out of date unless it is constantly and dramatically updated to conform. It seems much simpler to hold the transforms executed by the early layers to be constant.

The feature-encoded representation provides input to the ADB system in OVSIM. Memory units with 6, 8 or 10 inputs learn to map from this representation into output which is interpreted as a vote from each unit to attack or not attack to the current input pattern. Enough of each size of memory unit exist to cover all of the feature-encoded representation with 98% probability: they are 686 6-input units, 515 8-input units, and 414 10-input units, for a total of 1615. Connections from these units to the representation, like connections from the feature-encoding units to the raw input, are random but fixed throughout a simulation.

Each memory unit j is implemented as a PLN augmented with a buffer. The binary input to j forms an address add_j into the look-up table memory, and outputs 1 with a probability equal to the value stored in $loc_j[add_j]$. The summed output of all 1615 units generates a total V, which is then used to generate the output action for OVSIM as a whole, and to generate an attention value.

The summed output ranges as $0 \leqslant V \leqslant 1615$, and can therefore be interpreted as a strength of or confidence in the decision to attack. The probability of generating an attack output varies in a semi-linear fashion with V, as shown in Figure 6.5.

At the same time, V is used to assign an attention value to the current input image, according to the step function shown in Figure 6.6. Attention is highest for $600 \leqslant V \leqslant 850$ – the most random responses from the system. It decreases as V becomes more polarized – indicating confidence that attack will be rewarded or that it should be avoided. Once the results of an action are very sure (and V approaches 0 or 1615), there is little more to learn about that stimulus, and it is not so important that the system retain the pattern until reinforcement arrives. The curve in Figure 6.6 is skewed so that inputs which generate a low probability of attack always also generate non-zero attention – as, if an attack occurs to a pattern entailing negative reinforcement, there is obviously something more to be learned. Conversely, inputs with a high probability of attack are obviously well-learned, and generate zero attention so as not to take up any buffer space.

The buffer in each memory unit has capacity to store two of the previous

---

[1] Higher sensory cortex of adult animals can certainly reorganize. For example, an adult monkey trained to a fine pointing task will develop an enlarged cortical representation for the active finger (Blakemore, 1988), but this is on a much smaller scale, and at a later level of processing.

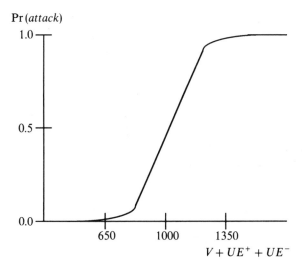

Figure 6.5 *The function used by OVSIM to convert votes V and unspecific effect components* UE^+ *and* UE^- *into probability of generating an attack input.*

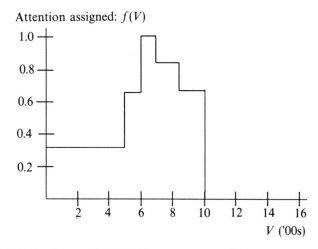

Figure 6.6 *The function used by OVSIM to convert votes V into attention to the current input pattern.*

input patterns add_j to that unit. If the new, current input is assigned a higher attention than that remaining to one of the buffered patterns, then it overwrites that buffered pattern. Attention decays linearly on each cycle, and so even if never overwritten, buffered patterns may only stay in the buffer for a finite period while their attention is non-zero; the decrement to attention is $\delta = 1/6$.

When reinforcement $r \in \{-1, 0, +1\}$ arrives, for each of the buffered elements with non-zero attention, the stored address X is reapplied to the look-up table, and the value $v_j = loc_j[att_j]$ addressed is adjusted as

$$\Delta v_j = 0.01r \qquad (6.1)$$

to a maximum of $v_j \leqslant 1.0$ and a minimum of $v_j \geqslant 0.0$.

It remains to define $\hat{s}$, the value to which the v_js are initialized at the start-up of a simulation. If $\hat{s} = 0.5$, approximately 50% of the 1615 memory units will output 1 in response to the first pattern – for a total of about 808. If the output-generating function is as defined above, then the probability of attack on a given cycle will be 0.15, while the probability of attack on a given trial (with a maximum of 20 cycles per trial) is then 0.96. This ensures that most new figures will be attacked on their first presentation, and agrees with the observation that an octopus generally does the same (Boycott and Young, 1956).

Recalling from Chapter 5 that the maximum delay bridgeable satisfies

$$f(\hat{s}) - (D - 1)\delta > 0 \qquad (6.2)$$

and that $\hat{s} = 0.5$ while by Figure 6.6, $f(0.5) = 1$, and that $\delta = 1/6$, the maximum delay bridgeable by this system is $D < 7$ cycles.

Finally, when the system outputs an attack decision, a sequence such as that shown in Figure 6.2 is initiated. At its termination, the appropriate reinforcement is elicited. If positive, the object remains out of sight as if ingested, while if negative, the object is 'released' and returns to its previous position. Reinforcement r once elicited occurs for 10 time cycles, after which r reverts to its resting value $r = 0$. Therefore, by Equation (6.1), each pattern in the buffer can receive a maximum of $+0.1$ or -0.1 reinforcement, and patterns with higher attention will be more strongly reinforced than those with attention which decays to zero in the meantime.

6.3 The unspecific effect

It may be noticed from Figure 6.5 that the system output generated is a function not only of V, the summed memory output, but also of UE^+ and UE^-. These parameters are the positive and negative components of the **unspecific effect** parameter.

In octopus, if a reinforcement is received after the animal attacks a stimulus object, the probability that the animal will attack the same figure on its next presentation is affected; this is the **specific effect** of training on the probability of attack. Simultaneously, if a positive reinforcement is received, the animal becomes noticeably more likely to attack *any* subsequent figure; after a negative reinforcement it is less likely to attack a subsequent figure. This is the **unspecific effect** of training. It is useful to decompose the unspecific effect into two components, the positive and negative, which increase and decrease respectively the overall probability of attack (Maldonado, 1963).

The unspecific effect is simulated in OVSIM by two parameters: UE^+, which increases after positive reinforcement, and UE^-, which increases after negative reinforcement. The system output is then calculated as in Figure 6.6 as a function of $V + UE^+ - UE^-$.

At rest, $UE^+ = UE_R^+ = 300$, while $UE^- = UE_R^- = 200$, so that there is a slight tendency to attack even in the absence of any reinforcement.[2] UE^+ increases immediately on receipt of a positive reinforcement by the system while UE^- increases after a negative one. The values of these parameters are calculated to decay logarithmically with the time since the last appropriate reinforcement

$$UE^+ (t) = \max \left[UE_R^+, UE_R^+ + 300 \left(1 - \ln \left(1 + 0.002 T^+\right)\right)\right] \qquad (6.3)$$

where T^+ is the number of cycles since the last positive reinforcement. Therefore, $UE^+ = 600$ when $T^+ = 0$, and decays to UE_R^+ within 900 cycles. Similarly

$$UE^- (t) = \max \left[UE_R^-, UE_R^- + 400\left(1 - \ln \left(1 + 0.002 T^-\right)\right)\right] \qquad (6.4)$$

where T^- is the number of cycles since the last negative reinforcement. Therefore, $UE^- = 600$ when $T^- = 0$, and decays to UE_R^- within 900 cycles. Notice that if positive and negative reinforcement occur within short spaces of each other, it is possible for both UE^+ and UE^- to be simultaneously inflated from their resting values.[3] Figure 6.7 shows the evolution of unspecific effect after reinforcement, and the average delay to attack an arbitrary object at various levels of unspecific effect.

In the literature dealing with octopus learning, the unspecific effect is at a maximum immediately after receipt of reinforcement, and declines logarithmically until probability of attack returns to the normal base level within one or two hours (Young, 1958b). Accordingly, unless the unspecific effect is itself an object of study, it is usual practice to pause between trials long enough to ensure that the unspecific effect is a negligible influence on training. For the OVSIM experiments reported in this chapter (but not in the next), a similar convention is followed, and enough cycles of inactivity pass between

[2] The choice of UE_R^+ larger than UE_R^- is in deference to the fact that upon removal of the brain centres in octopus believed responsible for the unspecific effect, a slight decrease in unspecific tendency to attack is observed (Young, 1964). This implies that, at rest, there is a slight net positive unspecific effect.

[3] The unspecific effect should decay within a time period equivalent to its decay schedule in octopus. The measure used here was this: since each octopus trial lasts for a maximum of e.g., two minutes (Young, 1964), while each OVSIM trial lasts for a maximum of twenty cycles, define one cycle to occupy 6 seconds of *simulated* time. Then, since the unspecific effect decays within 1–2 hours in octopus, it should also decay within the same amount of simulated time in OVSIM. Since 1.5 hours of simulated time entail 900 cycles, this was the time frame assigned for decay of unspecific effect on OVSIM.

(a.)

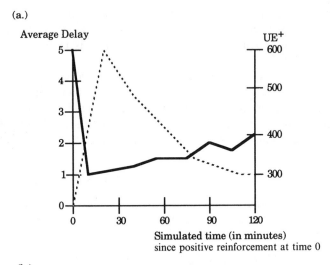

(b.)

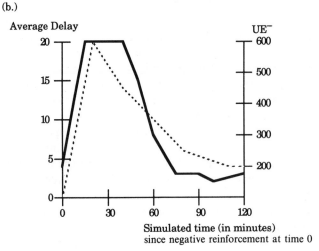

Figure 6.7 *Solid line shows the average delay to attack a random pattern after (a) positive or (b) negative reinforcement at time 0; dashed line shows evolution of (a) UE^+ or (b) UE^- after reinforcement at time 0.*

trials to decay UE^+ and UE^- to base levels. Therefore, for the remainder of this chapter, the unspecific effect is ignored.

6.4 Operant conditioning experiments with OVSIM

This section describes several experiments with OVSIM, under conditions meant to be analogous to operant conditioning tasks, specifically those documented with octopus. They consist essentially of learning whether or not to attack individual stimulus inputs: binary patterns for OVSIM, or visual images for octopus. It must be emphasized that any computer program learning simple – if delayed – associations carried out only a weak version of the task confronting an animal. For instance, it is a much more intricate operation to teach an octopus to fail to attack a crab, its natural food source, than any parallel operation in OVSIM. Nonetheless, the basic delay learning character of these tasks is comparable, and this justifies some relation of the learning curves of octopus and OVSIM.

6.4.1 Simple discrimination tasks

One task which the octopus learns fairly quickly is to discriminate between vertical and horizontal rectangular figures. These tend to be made of plastic, measuring about 5 cm, and are lowered into the far end of the tank on string or pieces of wire (Young, 1964). Each time the animal attacks the figure designated as positive, it is reinforced with a bit of food; attacks to the negative figure are punished with an electric shock. This may be delivered from a separate source applied to the octopus's skin, or the figure itself may be wired. Wells (1968) described experiments in which the octopuses could learn this task within about ten trials with each figure, in alternating presentation.

This kind of learning, **discrimination of neutral stimuli** which have no previous reinforcement value, is the simplest to simulate with a learning machine. OVSIM can be trained to discriminate between patterns showing horizontal and vertical bars (see Figure 6.1) within about 7.7 trials with each figure. An interesting aspect of studying machine learning is that, at the close of learning, it is possible to examine the units in a way that is not yet possible with neurons in the brain. The measure here which seems of particular utility is not the absolute frequency with which attacks occur to a stimulus, but the percentage response of memory units voting for attack to that pattern. Ideally, this should approach 100% for the positive figure and 0% for the negative one. In practice, these asymptotes may never be reached if the patterns are similar and their representations interfere. This is especially true since the input to the memory units is not the raw pattern, but its recoding in terms of feature-detector outputs. Figure 6.8 shows how the percentage response to the stimuli evolves as a function of trials in this task. Although the system response is accurate after about ten trials – that is, at least one attack output is generated within twenty cycles each time the positive pattern is presented, and none is generated within twenty cycles to the negative pattern – the probability of attack takes longer to converge. A nice feature of the curve shown in Figure 6.8 is the roughly decreasing acceleration of the positive curve; this is the same shape as the classic learning curve experienced in almost all learning experiments – with lower animals, primates and humans. The negative curve shows that the probability of attack declines from the initial low level.

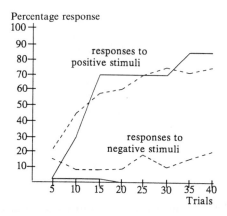

Figure 6.8 *Solid lines show the OVSIM response to positive vertical bar and negative horizontal bar stimuli, with alternating trials, as a function of trials. Each point is averaged from three simulations. Dashed line shows superimposed (and rescaled) shape of learning curve for octopus on similar task; dada averaged from 25 animals, after Young (1964).*

A different class of discrimination task involves training the octopus to attack a crab when presented alone, but not when shown together with a small plastic square. This task first involves teaching the animal not to attack its natural food source under some conditions; it also involves a learning set in which the negative pattern is a superset of the positive pattern. Boycott and Young (1955) found that octopuses could learn this discrimination within about ten days at three trials per day.

It is not really possible to replicate in OVSIM the concept of 'learning not to attack a natural food source'. However, it is possible to construct a training set in which the negative pattern subsumes the positive one. In these experiments, a crab pattern and crab-plus-square pattern are the training stimuli (refer to Figure 6.1). Of course the 'crab' pattern has no semantic value to OVSIM, but it makes discussion easier if the input patterns actually look like what they are meant to represent. It is also the case that the horizontal lines are good activators of OVSIM's feature detectors in much the same way that the horizontal legs of the crab may be good activators of the octopus's feature detectors (Young, 1964).

So, given the crab and crab-plus-square patterns, OVSIM can learn to distinguish between them within about ten trials with each.

The first important aspect of these results is that the OVSIM system can accomplish delay learning. It can learn to associate the original stimulus image with the eventual reinforcement, even when distracting images intervene. These intervening images are distracting not only because they are irrelevant, but also because there is a high degree of overlap between the intervening images during positive and negative trials, and therefore a high potential for interference between the positive and negative learning.

The next important aspect of these results is that a learning curve is generated, as in Figure 6.8, which is similar in shape to the learning curve obtained from animals. (Figure 6.8 shows a sample learning curve from an octopus during the horizontal-vertical discrimination overfitted.)

Finally, the time scale, in terms of numbers of presentations, is quite low – about ten exposures to each problem to be learned. In the language of artificial neural networks, this is remarkable speed, given that many training paradigms require hundreds or even thousands of presentations of each pattern.

6.4.2 Delay to attack stimuli

When the experimenter trains an octopus to attack stimuli in the tank, the animal at first only attacks after a long delay or observation period which may take several minutes (Young, 1964). Indeed, since most experimental octopuses have been captured rather than bred, there is a period of adjustment during which they must be 'retrained' to attack crabs. The delay to attack is apparent here as well as in experimental training circumstances. With repeated trials, the octopus gradually decreases both this delay and the overall time taken to carry out the attack. Eventually, as shown in Figure 6.9, the octopus will attack a crab or other positive figure as soon as it touches the tank floor (Young, 1964).

The converse occurs in learning to attack a negative figure. The initial delay gradually increases with negative reinforcement. Eventually, the delay will increase so far that the animal makes no attack within the two minutes maximum time cycle, and the trial is scored as a no-attack. However, attacks

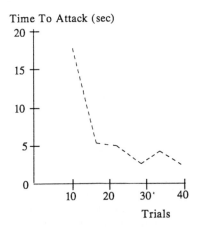

Figure 6.9 *The fall in delay to attack positive crab stimulus in octopus as a function of trials. Each point is averaged from ten animals, after Young (1964).*

never cease altogether in octopus, and if the negative stimulus is left in the field indefinitely, an attack will occur eventually (Muntz and Gwyther, 1988). This suggests that the process generating attacks in the animal is probabilistic: that positive reinforcement raises the probability of generating an attack until, shown the positive stimulus, the animal almost always attacks immediately; while, shown the negative, the probability of attack is so low that it takes many pollings of that system before an attack output is produced (Young, 1990, personal communication).

This is certainly the case in OVSIM: output is produced by repeated polling

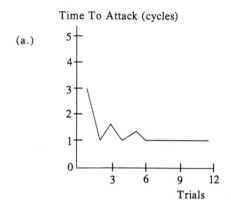

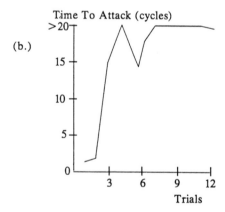

Figure 6.10 *(a) The fall in delay to attack a positive crab stimulus pattern in OVSIM as a function of trials. Each point is averaged from three simulations. (b) The rise in delay to attack a negative crab-plus-square stimulus pattern in OVSIM as a function of trials. Delay greater than 20 indicates no attack made within the 20 cycles constituting one trial. Each point is averaged from three simulations.*

(once per cycle) of the memory units, whose output produces a probability of attack. If this is high, attack will usually occur on the first cycle; if it is low but non-zero, it may take an indeterminate number of cycles before the generation of an attack output. This probabilistic basis gives rise to the same phenomenon of delay to attack as is observed in octopus.

Figure 6.10a shows the fall in delay to attack a positive stimulus in OVSIM; compared with Figure 6.9, there is a steep initial drop in the delay to attack, and this gradually decreases still further over succeeding trials to a minimum of attack on the first cycle in OVSIM and within the first few seconds in octopus. What is happening is that, on the first trial, when all memory units are outputting randomly, the probability of attack on any given cycle is 30% (refer Figure 6.5). Therefore, there is a 30% chance that an attack will occur on the first cycle, a 51% chance of an attack within the first two cycles, and so on. Figure 6.10 shows that, indeed, in most cases, an OVSIM will attack to a novel figure within an average of three cycles. Once this first attack occurs, positive reinforcement arrives and V is increased. This in turn increases the probability of attack on any given cycle and so decreases the average number of cycles elapsing before an attack is generated. Therefore, the delay to attack a positive stimulus decreases with training, as in the animal.

There is the related effect of increased delay to attack a negative stimulus in OVSIM as well, as Figure 6.10b shows. After the first attack (which occurs with the same probability as to the positive stimulus, since nothing is yet known about this new negative stimulus), V decreases. This in turn decreases the probability that an attack is generated on any given cycle within the next trial, and also increases the average delay to attack. When V falls to its minimum, the average delay to attack will have fallen also, hopefully to the point where the average delay is much longer than the 20 cycle limit on a trial, and OVSIM will have successfully learned not to attack that pattern.

6.4.3 Task interference and relearning

Interference between learning tasks was alluded to above; it refers to the situation where learning about one stimulus disrupts previous learning about a different stimulus, and affects the response output to that previous stimulus. If both stimuli are positive or both are negative, then the effect will be to improve the response to the previously learned stimulus. If, however, the stimuli differ in reinforcement value, the effect will be to degrade the previously learned response. This is a common effect in animal and human learning, and it occurs also in octopus. One interesting phenomenon concerns the re-learning of the appropriate response to the previously learned stimulus. It is often found that when the subject is retrained to respond appropriately to the previously learned (and interfered with) stimulus, the time to re-learn the response is significantly less than the time to learn the response in the first place, before interference. This implies that, even if the learned response is masked by interference, at least some of it remains in memory, and can be recovered in relearning trials.

Boycott and Young (1955) investigated interference and relearning in octopus, using the crab (positive) and crab-plus-square (negative) task. Each day, the animal was given three trials with the crab, which it was allowed to grasp and eat, followed by three with the negative stimulus and electric shock, if attacked. This routine was repeated for several days. On the first day, the delay to attack the positive stimulus decreased, indicating that the octopus was learning to attack it consistently. Then during the negative trials, the delay to attack increased as the animal learned about that stimulus. On the second day, Boycott and Young found interference had occurred to the positive stimulus: the response to the positive stimulus had decreased from its levels at the end of training with it on the previous day. During the three positive trials on the second day, the response increased to its previous strongest levels. Similarly, when the negative stimulus was presented on the second day, the response to it had increased, and re-learning occurred to decrease it. On the third day, interference had occurred again, but it was less strong than on the previous day, and re-learning was accomplished more quickly. This pattern was repeated on subsequent days, with the amount of re-learning necessary decreasing each day, indicating that there was saving of the learned information and that long-term memories were being formed which could at least partially survive the interference from the opposite stimulus and from the overnight pause in training.

This kind of experiment can be approximated in OVSIM using the crab and crab-plus-square patterns as positive and negative stimuli. The learning routine consists of alternating blocks of positive and negative trials. System response follows the same patterns as in the octopus. Again, it is more interesting to look at the *change* in the probability of response from OVSIM rather than the response itself. Figure 6.11 shows that within one block of positive trials, it has dropped, but regains its former level more quickly. On subsequent blocks of positive training, the initial positive response has not dropped so far as on the beginning of the previous day, and the final response within each block is a slight improvement over the last block. In the negative blocks, again, some learning is lost through interference during the positive blocks, but is regained and improved upon within each subsequent negative block.

OVSIM's memory is such that any positive reinforcement increases the probability of attacking an arbitrary figure. This is easy to see for an individual memory unit. At a given point in time, the probability that that memory unit will output an attack vote in response to a random input (and hence a random address) can be computed as

$$\Pr(\text{output} = 1) = \sum_{x=1}^{X} \Pr(x \text{ addressed}) v_x = \frac{1}{X} \sum_{x=1}^{X} v_x \qquad (6.5)$$

Pr(*attack*)

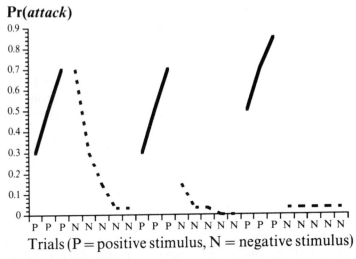

Trials (P = positive stimulus, N = negative stimulus)

Figure 6.11 *Learning and relearning in OVSIM with interleaved blocks of positive (crab pattern, solid line) and negative (crab-plus-square pattern, dashed line) trials. Each block of training interferes with opposite memory, but as learning proceeds the interference is less severe. Each point averaged from ten simulations; from Myers (1991b).*

When the response to a single input is reinforced positively, the value v_x stored at the location addressed by some input x, $1 \leqslant x = X$ is incremented by the rule in Equation (6.1). This change is enough to increase the probability of outputting an attack vote to a random pattern, as calculated by Equation (6.5).

In addition, because of the distributed nature of the memory units, there will also be interference between the specific positive and negative patterns involved. Each memory unit samples only a small portion (6 – 10 bits) of the input pattern. For some, the input on those bits will be the same for both the positive and negative patterns – since the positive and negative patterns in this task overlap at 88% of bits. Therefore, during a positive trial, the value addressed at those units will be increased, which in turn will serve to increase the probability of that unit outputting a 1 in response to the negative pattern which addresses that location as well. As the positive pattern is reinforced repeatedly over a block of trials, this effect can become strong enough to disrupt the negative response to the point shown in Figure 6.11. With additional blocks of training, however, the units which are addressed differently by the two patterns become very strongly disposed to output the appropriate response to each pattern. If enough of these units exist, they can overcome the fluctuating outputs of the overlapping units, and the system as a whole will produce the correct response.

6.4.4 Transfer of discrimination learning

In the same way as learning about a stimulus with opposite reinforcement value can cause interference to a previously learned stimulus, the previous learning can also influence the response to a novel stimulus. This occurs for exactly the same reasons as outlined in the previous section; it is just a case of viewing the phenomenon in the opposite direction. When previous learning affects the response to a new stimulus, the phenomenon is termed **transfer** of learned knowledge.

Boycott and Young (1955) conducted experiments in which octopuses, trained to attack one figure, were then presented with another. The animals were first trained to attack a crab shown alone but not when shown together with a white square. Then, they describe how the animals will also not attack if the crab is shown together with a circle or triangle equal in area to the square, or together with a square of area half the size of the original. One interpretation of this data is simply that the animals have learned the rule: attack the crab when alone, but not when shown with anything else. A second possible interpretation is that the feature-detecting cells in the octopus optic lobe encode all of the geometric shapes used in such a way that the memory system of the octopus produces the same response to all. This interpretation suggests that the octopus simply cannot discriminate easily between different geometric shapes. This is a fairly difficult question to resolve completely in octopus.

It is much easier to resolve in OVSIM, where each individual unit can be examined during and after learning. It is possible to determine exactly how the feature-detecting units will respond to any given stimulus pattern, and to predict how the system as a whole will respond – by comparing the output of the feature-detecting units with their outputs to the trained patterns.

In experiment, OVSIMs were trained to the crab versus crab-plus-square distinction. The systems were then presented with patterns containing the crab plus a smaller square, a circle, a reversed circle and a triangle. These stimuli are shown in Figure 6.12. For each new pattern, it is possible to compute the overlap with the negative and with the positive training patterns – in terms of the percentage of feature-detecting units which will respond the same way to the new and trained patterns. This is then a measure of the similarity of the input provided to the memory units. Figure 6.13 shows the results of this computation; it will be the same for all OVSIMs, since there is no randomness in the connections of the feature-detecting units to the raw data – only in the connections from these units to the memory units.

As seen in Figure 6.13, the OVSIMs should respond to the crab-plus-small-square in the same way as to the positive pattern, since the overlap between feature-detector outputs is much greater with the positive pattern than with the negative pattern. The response to the other three new patterns should be the same as to the negative pattern, as they have greater overlap. In fact,

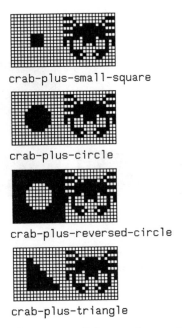

Figure 6.12 *Untrained patterns used for transfer experiments in OVSIM.*

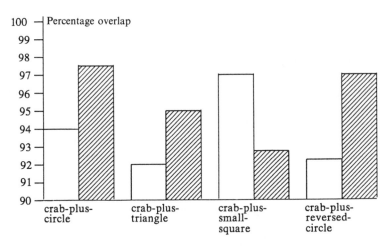

Figure 6.13 *Predicted transfer of learning in OVSIM; the percentage overlap of each untrained pattern with the trained crab (unfilled) and crab-plus-square (filled) patterns, in terms of duplicate response from feature-detectors.*

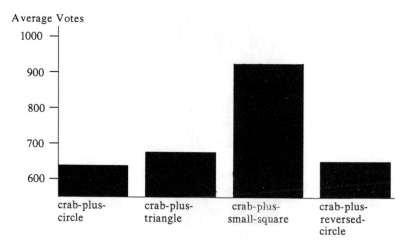

Figure 6.14 *Observed transfer of learning in OVSIM: the average votes from the memory units to each untrained pattern shows a clear attack tendency for the crab-plus-small-square pattern and clear no-attack tendencies for the other three. Each response is averaged from 15 simulations.*

in simulation, this is exactly what occurred. Figure 6.14 shows the average response of several OVSIM systems to the new patterns: the average response to the crab-plus-small-square pattern is a strong probability of attack, while the probability of attack is much weaker for the other three patterns. All four responses are well removed from the middle ground near an 800-vote response, which would signify no knowledge about the input. The system therefore shows transfer of learned patterns of response to new inputs.

This type of experiment also suggests a direction of animal research which might be very useful in determining how a species categorizes its inputs. If a computer system is devised with feature-detectors which very carefully parallel those in the animal, then the responses of the computer to new patterns should show the same transfer as in the animal. If the response of the computer differs from the animal, it is a good indication that the model of the animal's feature-detection system is incomplete or even inaccurate. This type of simulation work might turn out to be more expedient than the careful, laborious and large-scale single-cell recordings which are currently required to develop these models.

6.4.5 Tasks involving multiple discriminations

One of the most cognitively advanced experiments conducted with octopus involves multiple discriminations. Here, the animals learn the correct responses to a series of stimuli, rather than just two. The octopus can simultaneously remember at least six stimulus–response associations (Boycott and

Young, 1956). Boycott and Young first trained the animals to attack a small square but not a large one. Once this was learned, the trials with these stimuli were alternated with trials involving a positive vertical rectangle and a negative horizontal rectangle. When the animals could respond correctly to all four, training with a final pair of positive white circle and negative black circle was interleaved. Figure 6.15 shows how training progressed for one animal.

Boycott and Young make the following points about these data:

1. The second, vertical–horizontal discrimination takes some 40 trials to learn. Ordinarily, this is an easy task for the octopus to learn (Wells (1968) cites a learning time of about ten trials). Therefore, it takes longer to learn each association in a multiple discrimination task than to learn the same associations in a single discrimination task.

2. When the second, vertical–horizontal discrimination is introduced, the response to the first discrimination becomes less accurate. Errors are mostly failures to attack positive stimuli. Therefore, subsequent discrimi-nations interfere with learned ones, especially by inhibiting the attack response.

3. After this interference, the first discrimination never quite regains its accuracy. Therefore, there must be competition for memory space, which intensifies as more memories are acquired.

4. Adding the third, white–black discrimination interferes little with the accuracy of response to the previous two. Young (1964) hypothesizes that this is because contrast discrimination is recorded within the memory

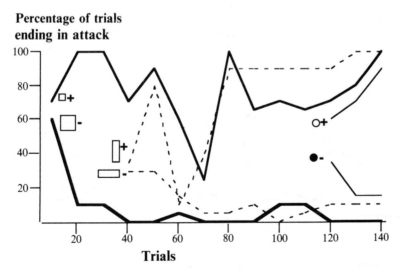

Figure 6.15 *Multiple discrimination learning in a single octopus, after Young (1964).*

system by a different set of cells from those encoding shape discrimination. Another possibility is that once the two discriminations find mutually compatible storage arrangements, they are sufficiently stable not to be disrupted by new memories.

5. Eventually, all six stimuli elicit mainly correct responses, indicating that the octopus visual memory system is capable of storing at least six associations simultaneously.

Interestingly, several of the points made by Boycott and Young about multiple discrimination learning in octopus also apply to multiple discrimination learning OVSIM. To replicate this task in OVSIM, the system was first well trained (over 15 trials) to attack a vertical bar pattern but not a horizontal one. Then training with a negative large square and positive small square was added. A further ten trials sufficed for the average response to all inputs to be correct. Finally, training with a positive circle and negative reversed circle was added. After ten more trials with each of the six stimuli, the system was responding correctly to each. Figure 6.16 shows the six stimuli and the evolution of responses within the system to each.

It is to be expected that the memory units in OVSIM, with nothing else to store except these experiments, would be capable of storing six associations simultaneously. In fact they are. At the end of training, each positive stimulus was attacked with a probability of at least 70% on each cycle, while the probability of attacking each negative pattern was at most 3% on any cycle.

The other points made by Boycott and Young deserve rather more discussion within the context of OVSIM.

1. The time for OVSIM to learn the second, vertical–horizontal discrimination averages 10.0 attacks or 11.0 trials with each stimulus. This is significantly longer than the average 7.67 trials required for a naive OVSIM to learn the same task. Like in octopus, it takes longer for OVSIM to find a

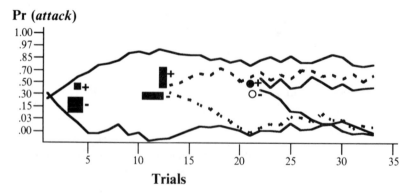

Figure 6.16 *Multiple discrimination learning in OVSIM; each point is average response in votes from five simulations.*

memory representation compatible with four simultaneous images than with two.

2. Introduction of the second discrimination to OVSIM does disrupt the previous knowledge, as shown in Figure 6.16 by slight returns to randomness in the response to the first two patterns when the next two are introduced. The average response to the vertical rectangle falls from 70% to 66%, while that to the horizontal rectangle rises from 33% to 35%. Both are small trends, but both are statistically significant (by t-test).

3. In octopus, the response to the first discrimination never again regains its full strength after the second discrimination is introduced. The responses in OVSIM also show a slightly stronger level just before the introduction of the second discrimination, which is never again quite regained. However, the effect is not nearly so pronounced as in the animal. The suggestion is either that the OVSIM memory has a higher capacity (given that it has nothing else to store but this task), or that the encoding of the stimuli in OVSIM is such as to minimize interference from the second discrimination on the memory for the first. A final possibility is that the octopus also, given longer training time, would have been able to recover the original strength of its memories.

4. Addition of the third discrimination interferes little with the performance to the previous two in OVSIM, as in octopus. There is a slight disruption to all responses, but t-test shows that only the response to the negative horizontal pattern suffers statistically significant disruption. Young (1964) attributes the lack of interference in octopus to the difference in coding memories about shape versus coding those about contrast or colour: he suggests that the first two discriminations would be encoded in a physically different region of memory from the third one. However, this is not really the case in OVSIM. Rather than recognizing a qualitative difference in the kind of memory to be stored, the memories in OVSIM become progressively more fixed with training, and so the introduction of a new stimulus to be learned cannot disrupt them. Instead, the response for the new pattern must be stored among whatever memory is left unused. This, in memory unit terms, will be the number of units in which the new pattern addresses a location not used by any other pattern of opposite reinforcement value. In only this sense is the black–white discrimination stored in a 'different' kind of memory. This also explains why successive discriminations are learned with successively less strength: less memory is available to encode them.

6.5 OVSIM as an operant conditioning model

This chapter has attempted to show how an ADB-based system, OVSIM, can be applied to operant conditioning tasks. These have been modelled on operant conditioning data obtained from studies with octopus, because that data is plentiful and because the animal is fairly simple, but in fact the basic task is comparable to the general formalization of operant conditioning, of which octopus learning is only one example.

Obviously, OVSIM can make no claim to model even the octopus visual discrimination learning system in all its complexity, much less to approach the sophistication of a brain which, at the same time as it is solving laboratory problems, is also regulating bodily functions, considering the effects of hunger, paranoia, and even depression, and preparing itself for the onset of the next mating season. These are effects for which laboratory experiments try to control, but they are certainly present nonetheless.

Still, the tasks outlined above for OVSIM maintain the essential features of operant conditioning: reinforcement is non-specific and arrives contingent on the production of some response and with some inherent (although possibly short) delay. The fact that the learning curves and other behaviours obtained from OVSIM are in many cases closely correlated with the results obtained from a particular animal, the octopus, suggest that there may be a case for exploring learning in that particular animal with reference to the strategies in OVSIM. It is to this kind of experiment that the next chapter turns.

7

OVSIM and the octopus: the case for modelling

In Chapter 6, the ADB-based system OVSIM was applied to a series of operant conditioning experiments. These were taken from data covering the performance of the octopus learning visual discrimination tasks, but the point was made that they represent fairly standard operant conditioning tasks, and in that sense the particular animal giving rise to the data was unimportant.

However, because of the close correspondence obtained between the OVSIM and octopus in terms of learning curves, it is intriguing to consider the possibility that OVSIM can be useful as a model of the portion of octopus brain which oversees this learning. There has been a great deal of work done on damage experiments with octopus: recording learning or performance impairment when various regions of the brain are ablated or otherwise damaged. The regions damaged are implicated by default in the behaviours which cease to appear after the damage. Therefore, it is possible to assign specific functions, within the operant conditioning task, to various regions of the octopus brain. These regions can then be mapped loosely to the components of OVSIM which perform analogous functions.

One way of investigating the accuracy of this mapping is to consider damage experiments with OVSIM: when a component of OVSIM is 'damaged', does the remaining system show deficits comparable to those observed in octopus after damage to the brain region to which it has been mapped? The experiments considered in this chapter show that there is in fact a good degree of correspondence between damaged OVSIM and octopus. As a result, OVSIM can provide constructive support for the hypotheses which assign particular functions to particular brain regions in the animal.

7.1 An overview of the octopus visual learning system

In order to compare the modules of octopus brain with the modules of OVSIM, it is first necessary to review some basics of the anatomy of the octopus visual learning system, and the range of tasks to which it is known to be trainable.

Anatomically, the octopus has a reasonably sophisticated nervous system consisting of some 500 million nerve cells. The particular suitability of the octopus for study is due in large part to the fact that the motor processes and sensory processes are kept largely separate: over 300 million of these neurons are distributed among the arms, where they control delicate movements and intricate somatosensory explorations. The ganglia overseeing reflex reactions are located in the arms as well. Thus, only some 2×10^8 nerve cells are centralized within the 'brain'; even within this central area, some 50 subregions form well-defined lobes, with limited interlobe connections.

A further advantage of studying the octopus is that its behaviours are quite stylized. *Octopus vulgaris*, the common octopus found in the waters near Naples, lives in crannies on the ocean floor. In the experimental tank, a pile of bricks can provide a makeshift 'home'. From the home, the octopus extends an arm to seize crabs swimming by. If the crab is out of immediate reach, the octopus may jet out, seize the prey, and return to cover. The captured meal is paralysed with a salivary secretion, broken up by beak and radula, and passed into the mouth. Life for the octopus consists in large part of repeated decisions about whether to attack objects moving within the visual field.

Other behaviours occur in these animals, including mating, locomotion and orientation, posturing at rivals, conditioned responses to touch stimuli (another topic of intensive study), and complex skin patterning for camouflage or to accompany courtship displays and defence attitudes. Some species of octopus even engage in complex social organization (Mather, 1982, 1985) and migration in search of homes (Hartwick *et al.*, 1984). Only conditioned learning about attack decisions for visual stimuli is considered here.

The naive (untrained) octopus has an innate tendency to attack moving objects in the visual field, but it will seldom attack stationary ones (Muntz and Gwyther, 1988). Usually the initial response to a strange moving object is attack after a considerable delay, as shown in Figure 6.9; if the object turns out to be edible, the delay quickly disappears on subsequent trials. Without positive reinforcement, hesitation becomes even more prolonged until attacks die away altogether (Young, 1964). Objects which can be trained in this way include black and white geometric shapes (Young, 1964), objects at different contrast (Young, 1968), and sinusoidal gratings of discriminable frequencies (Muntz and Gwyther, 1988). Maldonado (1963) describes experiments where octopuses were conditioned successfully to discriminate on the basis of movement, brightness, direction of movement in relation to the long axis of a geometric figure or in relation to the points of a shape, territory, vertical or horizontal extent of a figure, and analysis of contour. While octopuses are apparently not sensitive to colour (Young, 1964), Wells (1968) notes that octopuses "have elaborate eyes and can learn to distinguish most of the differences between shapes that are apparent to us".

There is automatic transfer of learning between visual fields; so that an octopus which learns about an object presented to one eye alone, will respond appropriately if that object is then presented to the other eye.

An important inability of the visual learning system is the lack of generalization over size. At least in the octopus, size generalization is not conferred automatically during learning, so that an object seen at one size or one distance may not be recognized if enlarged, or moved farther away. The fact that an octopus knows to attack a crab wherever in the visual field it appears seems to be a result of learning with the crab figure at various retinal sizes during the octopus's approach to the food object. Young (1964) has shown that a trained animal does not recognize a stimulus when doubled or halved in size, and is even less likely to recognize the object when the viewing distance is altered significantly.

The octopus retina consists of an array of photo-receptor cells which, unlike our own, are oriented toward the light (Young, 1971). The cells are arranged in a rectangular grid, and show vertical and horizontal axes (Young, 1964), perhaps giving the first indications of why vertical and horizontal discriminations should be preferentially easy for the animals to learn. There are no other neurons within the retina, and so it is the axonal processes of these same receptors which form the optic nerves exiting the eye. The optic nerves cross in the optic chiasm, and travel to innervate the contralateral optic lobes, two structures lying just behind the eyes in octopus.

The optic lobes subserve two critical functions: first, they are believed to be the seat of visual memory storage in octopus. Second, the optic lobes are responsible for outputs to the motor system which initiate attack and retreat patterns; they also participate in a visual feedback loop with other centres to fine-tune motor actions (Young, 1971). Together, the optic lobes contain some 92% of the neurons within the central nervous system (Young, 1964).

The outer layer of the optic lobe receives visual information in a relatively unprocessed state, and is thought to consist of cells which classify visual input in terms of features such as brightness, horizontal and vertical edge, movement, etc. (Young, 1971). The dendritic fields of these cells are regular in shape and mostly oval (Young, 1971), which suggests that they act as shape and orientation filters; most are horizontally or vertically elongated, which may well be another factor aiding the octopus in learning horizontal and vertical discrimination (Young, 1971).

The cells of the optic lobe interior receive input from these classifying cells, but show no distinct field shapes or topographic mapping (Young, 1971). They therefore receive information about widely varying regions of the visual field. These are the cells which, it is supposed, adapt their output appropriately to visual stimuli. They often show two or more axons, which then leave the optic lobe for the motor centres, where they play a role in the initiation of patterns of motor behaviour.

Vision in the octopus is basically monocular – the visual fields observed by

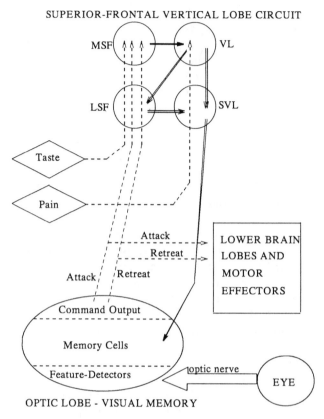

SUPERIOR-FRONTAL VERTICAL LOBE CIRCUIT

OPTIC LOBE - VISUAL MEMORY

Figure 7.1 *Schematic diagram of the regions of octopus brain involved in visual attack learning: MSF = median superior frontal lobe; LSF = lateral superior frontal lobe; VL = vertical lobe; SVL = subvertical lobe, from Myers (1991b) after Boycott (1967), Wells (1959) and Young (1971).*

the two eyes are mostly non-overlapping – and so each optic lobe gives rise to an independent motor command to attack or retreat. The decisions from the lobes may conflict, and this conflict must be resolved either in the motor centres or elsewhere.

In addition to the motor centres, the output of the optic lobes also travels to the higher lobes: the median superior frontal, lateral superior frontal, vertical and subvertical lobes, as shown in Figure 7.1. Together, these four lobes form the superior-frontal–vertical lobe (SFVL) circuit, which contains internal cyclic pathways and also reciprocal connection to the optic lobe. Additional input to the SFVL circuit comes from sensors for taste and pain: the reinforcement from an attack action.

The SFVL circuit combines taste and pain (positive and negative reinforcement) to suppress or amplify tendencies for the optic lobe signal to attack (Young, 1964). It also aids in the setting up of optic lobe memories according to the reinforcement of taste and pain (Young, 1964). Its own output does not seem to be altered by long-term experience.

Most information about the specific functioning of the lobes comes from ablation experiments: an animal, naive or trained to some discrimination, has one or more lobes removed, and the function of the missing areas can be deduced from the resulting behavioural changes. The effects are often complex, as other factors come into play such as postsurgical shock and loss of input to otherwise intact nearby brain regions. In particular, any ablation of SFVL tissue interrupts both a self-re-exciting chain and also a loop with the optic lobe: thus there may well be loss of function only indirectly related to the ablated tissue.

Consensus is that the superior frontals serve to increase the tendency to attack, particularly for distant objects which the octopus must jet out to reach (Young, 1970).

The vertical lobe is thought to serve a complementary function: to integrate the effects of pain, and where appropriate to use them to repress attacking. Its removal leads to a plethora of related effects. The primary among these seems to be the inability to learn avoidance behaviours. Learned responses are maintained intact – the octopus will still avoid objects it previously learned not to attack – but it cannot learn not to attack a new object associated with electric shock (Young, 1964), particularly if it is an object the octopus is innately predisposed to attack, like a crab (Young, 1970). Removing the vertical lobe also results in a reduced level of non-specific tendency to attack.

The subvertical lobe provides the system's feedback output to the optic lobes. It combines the amplification and suppression of the other lobes: in effect, it passes through the signals from the superior frontals unless the vertical lobe intervenes with restraining signals (Young, 1964). Again, a principal effect of the ablation of this lobe is a non-specific reduction in the tendency to attack (Young, 1971).

Research on the octopus learning centres is ongoing, and the assignation of function to the four higher lobes of the SFVL circuit is still a matter of hypothesis rather than fact. In particular, there is strong evidence that the median superior frontal plays a much more complex role than the account above would suggest (Young, 1990, personal communication), but it is not yet completely characterized. However, in a sense this is a matter for the biologist which is only indirectly related to the current modelling problem. Learning in OVSIM should model the *function* of the higher lobes; it is not concerned with the *distribution* of this function among its four subregions. This would require a much finer grained model and one specialized to imitate the octopus brain. It will be enough to show that a subset of OVSIM behaves in a manner analogous to the higher brain centres in octopus.

There is no evidence (Young, 1964) that the centres of the SFVL circuit learn with experience or alter with satiation or hunger. Instead, they seem to deal with changes in the tendency to attack, and also seem to be involved in the assignment of reinforcement information to memories within the optic lobes. It is believed that the SFVL is further involved in the transfer of learned knowledge from one to the opposite optic lobe. An octopus with training in one visual field, and hence in one optic lobe, can solve the same problems if presented to the other visual field (Young, 1964); an animal without the vertical lobe cannot do this.

It seems likely that the long-term visual memories are stored within the optic lobes. The SFVL circuit may maintain short-term memories until reinforcement arrives and then pass these memories on to the optic lobes for permanent storage there. Alternatively, short-term memories may be stored within the optic lobe, but the SFVL may be responsible for setting up these short-term memories or for overseeing their eventual transference into long-term memory.

7.2 OVSIM as a model of the octopus visual attack learning system

The above discussion makes it clear that the octopus visual attack learning system, consisting principally of the optic lobes and SFVL circuit, is responsible for at least one type of operant conditioning. Research has suggested that the optical lobes from the system's associative memory (i.e., initiating a conditioned motor response to a given visual input), while the SFVL circuit is responsible for maintenance of short-term memories in the period between their execution and the reinforcement they elicit. It may accomplish this by operating as a buffer, or by controlling a buffer in the optic lobe, or perhaps in another manner altogether.

In this role, the SFVL seems to perform the same function as the ADB mechanisms in OVSIM: that of bridging the delay between action and reinforcement. The optic lobes relate to that part of OVSIM which constitutes its associative memory. This means that the remaining functions of attention-setting, buffering and read-out of buffered memories into the long-term storage of the associative memory would have to depend on the operations of the SFVL.

In order to determine whether OVSIM without these functions shows performance deficits related to those in octopus with ablated lobes, various parts of the ADB system can be disabled.

In the worst case, if all of these functions depend critically on the SFVL, the ablation is equivalent to eradicating all function from the visual attack learning system except for simple association of simultaneously available input, action and reinforcement.

To achieve this in OVSIM, three alterations are necessary. First, the buffer is restricted to hold only a single element. Second, the attention-setting mechanism is restricted to output a constant function. Together, these two considerations ensure that the only pattern available when reinforcement arrives is the single most recent input. In other words, buffering is recency-driven rather than attention-driven, and buffering is very short-lived. The third alteration is to the unspecific effect mechanism. In octopus, the removal of the vertical lobe tends to increase the level of non-specific attack, while the removal of the lateral superior lobes tends to lower the level of non-specific attack. Therefore, in OVSIM, the removal of the vertical lobe is also defined as a replacement of UE^- with a constant, zero-valued signal, while the removal of the lateral superior would be defined as setting UE^+ to a constant zero-valued signal.

With these alterations in place, resulting in what will be termed a 'damaged' OVSIM, it is possible to run experiments paralleling those set to damaged octopuses and compare the results. If the results are analogous, then this supports the idea that it is exactly those functions eliminated from OVSIM which are performed by the ablated brain regions in octopus.

7.3 Damage learning experiments

Damage learning experiments in octopus can take place in two ways, depending on the sequencing of lobe removal (R) and training (T) sessions. In the R–T paradigm, naive animals are first operated on, and then trained (as best as possible) to the discrimination task. In the T–R–T paradigm, the animals are first trained to successfully execute the task; then the operation is performed, and their subsequent performance on the same task is measured. The R–T paradigm investigates an animal's ability to *acquire* a task given the dysfunction of some brain regions, while the T–R–T paradigm investigates its ability to *perform* or *retain* a learned behaviour with the dysfunction. In the octopus experiments described here, all damage concerned the ablation of the vertical lobe, but both R–T and T–R–T paradigms were used.

A straightforward experiment with either R–T or T–R–T octopuses is to investigate their ability to acquire or retain the same kind of learning as described in Chapter 4: discrimination in attacking various figures. A dramatic change in the behaviour of R–T animals is their inability to learn to avoid attacking crabs (Young, 1970): typically, the R–T octopus stops attacking after receiving a shock, but 1–2 trials later it will again try attacking the stimulus. It will also be unable to learn discriminations involving crabs – such as to attack a crab unless shown together with a square (Boycott and Young, 1955). As described in the previous chapter, this is normally a straightforward task for the octopus to learn, even though it does involve the animal's natural food source.

Learning about neutral stimuli (such as plastic rectangular shapes) is also severely impaired in R–T animals. There is little evidence of learning within the few dozen trials normally needed for the octopus to master this task. There may be some slight difference in the probability of attack to the positive and negative stimuli after very lengthy training; for example, Young (1958a) found that after 180 trials, the animals would attack the positive stimulus five times more often than the negative.

The conclusion is that, in an octopus without the vertical lobe, there is little or no ability to express learning about non-neutral stimuli such as crabs, and only slight expression of learning about neutral stimuli after very long training. Tasks such as these throw little light on the question of whether the animals are unable to form new memories, unable to access them, or unable to express them.

If, for example, the R–T octopus is unable to form new memories, but can still access and express ones formed before the ablation, then a T–R–T octopus should still be able to perform learned discriminations well. However, Boycott and Young (1955) found that was not an accurate description of the situation. They first trained octopuses to the crab versus crab-plus-square discrimination, then ablated all vertical lobe tissue, and then retested the animals, finding that the memory preventing attack to the negative figure was lost and could not be reacquired. They found further that if only 30% of the lobe was removed, the animals performed as normal, while with increasing amounts of damage, the performance degraded gradually until by 80% removal the animal was unable to learn.

On the other hand, T–R–T octopuses can retain neutral discriminations quite well (Boycott and Young, 1956): typically, performance loses some accuracy immediately after vertical lobe removal, but the animals can slowly re-learn the task. They also found that disruption was worse for 'hard' discriminations than for 'easy' ones such as vertical versus horizontal bar discrimination. Boycott and Young (1956) suggested that memories for 'hard' discriminations are weaker before the operation, and therefore less likely to withstand it. This may also be the reason that the crab discriminations are heavily disrupted: this must be a 'hard' task for the animal to learn, as it involves not attacking a food item, and therefore the memory may be particularly weak and little able to withstand loss of part of the memory system.

A slightly different possibility is that the primary reason for the post-ablation disruptions is the loss of UE^- inhibiting attack to the negative figure.

Ordinarily, OVSIM can learn the crab versus crab-plus-square discrimination within some 10–15 trials (see section 5.4.1). Four R – T OVSIMs, disabled as described above before training, were still regularly attacking the negative pattern as well as the positive by the 25th trial. This is due to the huge increase in non-specific tendency to attack in the absence of UE^-. In the long term, such R–T OVSIMs did show some learning: a decrease from 100% attacks on the negative figure during the first five trials to an 80% attack rate by trials 20–25. The average response in votes to the negative pattern dropped to 30% during this period, which would have been sufficient to eliminate attacks in a normal OVSIM; but when this was augmented with UE^+ in the absence of UE, attacking continued. In the case of these simulations, the memory could be well *acquired*, indicated by the low vote response, but could not be *expressed* in the absence of UE^-.

A similar result is obtained with T–R–T OVSIMs. Four simulations, trained to the crab versus crab-plus-square task and then damaged, would then attack every pattern presented. Even after 20 cycles of training there was no improvement. Much of this failure is attributable to overwhelming non-specific tendency to attack, as in the R–T animals.

However, comparing the response in votes to the positive and negative patterns in the T–R–T simulations with those from the R–T ones shows that a somewhat stronger memory exists in the former. The average response to the positive pattern in the T–R–T simulations, at 61% of votes, is slightly but significantly higher than that in the R–T simulations. The average response to the negative pattern, at 28% of votes in the T–R–T simulations, is likewise significantly lower than in the R–T simulations. This means that there is a small saving of information in the T–R–T paradigm, and in turn means that after the OVSIM is damaged, it loses some of its ability to *acquire* knowledge as well as to express it.

This correspondence in observable behaviour between OVSIM and octopus is by no means sufficient to conclude that the mechanisms giving rise to this behaviour in OVSIM are similar to those in octopus. More support comes from the means in which R–T deficits can be overcome both in OVSIM and in the octopus.

Boycott and Young (1955) found that it is possible to reduce the tendency to attack the negative crab-plus-square stimulus in R–T octopuses – if the negative stimulus is left moving in the visual field after the administration of reinforcement. Normally, the stimulus is removed once the attack and reinforcement conclude. However, Boycott and Young suggested that when the stimulus is left visible after reinforcement, the octopus is more able to associate the stimulus with the reinforcement; this in turn suggests that learning takes place for a few seconds following reinforcement, and that the vertical lobe is normally responsible for providing a memory of the stimulus during this period (Boycott and Young, 1955). Therefore, R–T octopuses are unable to learn the association, but if the stimulus is left moving in the visual field, it is still available from the current visual inputs – and can be associated with the reinforcement in that way. For example, if the stimulus was left visible after an attack, it was not attacked again for up to seven minutes; while if it was removed from the tank and replaced after a shorter interval, the animal would attack it (Boycott and Young, 1955).

This idea is interesting in its relation to OVSIM. In OVSIM, vertical lobe ablation is simulated by, among other things, the elimination of attention-driven short-term buffering of inputs. The resulting system can only associate a reinforcement with the input pattern which immediately preceded it. Since reinforcement occurs for a number of cycles after an attack (see section 6.2), the damaged OVSIM will only be able to associate the reinforcement with the inputs current during those cycles. Since the trials are usually separated by 900 cycles, to allow UE^+ and UE^- to return to resting values, all but the first of these subsequent inputs will be blank, if the stimulus is negative; all will be blank if the stimulus is positive as Figure 6.2 shows. The result will be very limited learning as described in the previous section.

However, in octopus, if the blank visual field is replaced by the stimulus in the period just following attack, learning improves. This can be accomplished in OVSIM by replacing the inputs following attack with the original stimulus pattern. In this paradigm, the damaged OVSIM can learn even slightly faster than the normal OVSIM: because now, instead of having to wait until attention to the original stimulus is high enough that it remains in the buffer until reinforcement arrives, the original stimulus image is the only one available at reinforcement.

A slightly differing strategy in octopus to improve learning is continuous training. Ordinarily an interval of an hour or two is allowed between trials; however T–R–T animals have been tested with an interval of only five minutes between trials (Young, 1964). With this reduced interval, the animals did show learning after ablation. Possibly, in the absence of the vertical lobe, the memory tends to fade away quickly, but can be re-strengthened if the image again falls upon the retina. Figure 7.2 shows an example of learning with vertical lobe ablation; given closely spaced trials, the animal shows more improvement with time.

In OVSIM it is also possible, to a large extent, to improve learning with closely spaced trials. If trials are continuous – that is, after an attack, the

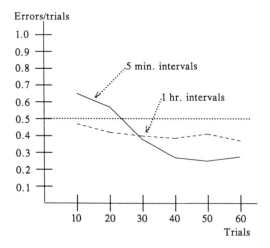

Figure 7.2 *Re-learning of horizontal versus vertical bar discrimination by octopus after vertical lobe removal, with five minute or one hour intervals between trials, after Young (1964).*

stimulus is left moving in the visual field until another attack occurs – the probability of attack falls much lower than when trials are separated by the normal 900 cycles or 1.5 hours of simulated time. The reason is that, like in the previous experiments, the reinforcement which is available for several cycles comes to be associated with the current input pattern: which in this case will be the correct original stimulus albeit from another trial. As a result, the system will learn not to attack the stimulus pattern.

Figure 7.3 shows learning of this task in three damaged OVSIMs with continuous trials and with normally-spaced trials. When 1200 cycles separate trials, there is some learning, as evidenced in a fall in the response in votes to the pattern, but it stabilizes at a level of about 455 votes. If the trials are continuous, the response can drop so low that the probability of attack is effectively 0, even in the absence of UE^- to counterbalance UE^+.

In Figure 7.3, the simulations receiving normally-spaced trials initially show faster learning than those receiving continuous trials, as evidenced in a more rapid drop in the average response in the first dozen or so trials. This is because the continuous system can attack on literally the next cycle after its last attack – while reinforcement is still present. In this condition, the prior reinforcement will be interrupted while the new one arrives. Therefore, the system may receive less reinforcement per attack than if trials were normally-spaced: in which case it would always receive a fixed number of cycles of

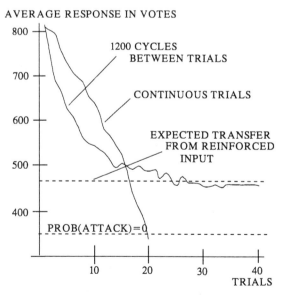

Figure 7.3 *Learning of crab versus crab-plus-square discrimination by OVSIM after 'damage', with normally-spaced or continuous trials, from Myers (1991b).*

negative reinforcement after each attack. Because, in damaged OVSIMs, the non-specific tendency to attack is so strong in the absence of UE^-, this continual attack behaviour occurs for at least the first few trials, until the level of response drops enough that there is usually some delay between attacks. When this begins to occur, the full ten cycles of reinforcement are experienced between attacks, and the simulations can catch up in learning with those simulations undergoing normally-spaced trials.

A second point about the learning shown in Figure 7.3 is that the apparent learning by simulations in the normally-spaced trials is really artifact. In the attack to a negative crab-plus-square pattern, as shown in Figure 6.2, the square is still present when reinforcement arrives. In the damaged OVSIMs, only able to buffer the last input pattern at each cycle, it is this pattern which will be present during the first cycle of reinforcement, and it is to this and the subsequent blank patterns that the reinforcement will be associated. Therefore, what looks like learning by the systems to the original stimulus image is merely transfer from what has been learned about the square pattern visible at the end of an attack. The overlap between the square pattern and the original crab-plus-square pattern is some 89%, in terms of the response of the feature-detecting units in OVSIM. From this, it is possible to calculate the expected response in votes to the crab-plus-square pattern, given that OVSIM has learned to reject the square pattern. This response will be proportional to the probability that each memory unit sees the same inputs from each pattern: for example, the probability that one of the 686 6-input memory units sees the same input from both patterns is 0.89^6. Therefore, the expected total number of memory units seeing the same input is

$$686(0.89)^6 + 515(0.89)^8 + 414(0.89)^{10} = 673 \qquad (7.1)$$

Each of these 673 units will output 0 for both patterns. Since the remaining units address new locations, which will still be initialized to output randomly when addressed, about half will also output 0. Therefore, the number of memory units expected to output 1 to the crab-plus-square pattern is

$$0.5 \times (1615 - 673) = 471 \qquad (7.2)$$

The upper dashed line in Figure 7.3 shows the level of an average response to 471 votes; while the actual average response of the OVSIMs with normally-spaced training was 455 of a possible 1615 votes.

These two points about Figure 7.3 relate to the octopus learning shown in Figure 7.2. First, the octopus learning in the 5-minute interval case starts off more slowly than that in the normally-spaced trials. Secondly, there is actually some slight improvement even in the normally-spaced trials, even though the eventual level reached is the same as the pre-operation response of the animal to a random pattern.

The fact that both OVSIM and octopus do show post-damage learning when trials are closely spaced in time suggests that OVSIM can provide an alternative hypothesis for the phenomenon in octopus. Rather than the vertical lobe providing non-specific refreshment to the images stored within the optic lobe (as suggested by Boycott and Young, 1955), or solely providing UE^- – a possibility mentioned by Young, (1958a) – it is possible that the vertical lobe is responsible for overseeing or maintaining an ADB-like function. The most critical part of its role would be the selection, via attention-setting, of which patterns should be best placed to compete for buffer space. After removal of the vertical lobe, by this hypothesis, the animal loses its ability to buffer any but the immediately preceding information. The OVSIM experiments show that this type of damage is sufficient to give rise to effects like those shown in octopus after vertical lobe ablation. It remains to be seen if it is possible to discriminate between these hypotheses in such a way as to settle the question concerning the function of vertical lobe in octopus.

Before leaving the topic of vertical lobe ablation, it is perhaps wise to mention the involvement of the lobe in a second learning system in octopus: the touch learning system. It was to the study of this system that Young and his co-researchers turned much of their attention throughout the 1970s. Discrimination learning in the touch system is quite comparable to that in the visual system. When the octopus is presented with a textured object placed against its arm, its innate reaction is to grasp it and draw it into the mouth; if it is inedible the octopus will eventually release it, and sometimes even push it away to arm's length. If the inedible object is repeatedly presented at short intervals, the time taken to examine it before rejection falls, until the object is rejected immediately upon presentation – usually within some three to five trials (Wells and Wells, 1957).

After vertical lobe removal, there is little difference in the ability to learn to reject an object; however, in a discrimination task – where positive and negative objects are presented alternately during learning – there is markedly more time required by the damaged animals, particularly as the discriminations become harder. Wells and Wells (1957) also found that relative performance of the damaged animals became worse when the frequency of training decreased. Since the damaged animals improved when trials were given at short intervals, it appears that the vertical lobe plays the same role in learning tactile discriminations as in learning visual ones: namely, affecting the retention of associations between trials.

This has interesting implications for the idea that the octopus carries out ADB: attention-driven buffering within a single modality might have a buffer specific to inputs from that modality, but it would require identical attention-setting mechanisms as all the other modalities which also perform ADB. If the vertical lobe provides this mechanism for visual learning in octopus, then it is sensible that the touch learning system should take advantage of it as well for its own purposes. Therefore, vertical lobe removal would imply similar impairment in both the visual and touch learning systems.

7.4 Another model of the octopus visual learning system

In the context of considering OVSIM as a model of the visual attack learning system of octopus, it can also be compared with an early model of the same system developed by Maldonado several decades ago. His model is a block-diagram of a system capable of learning to produce attack and retreat responses to visual patterns, but is meant to be consistent with the known biology of the learning system in octopus. Figure 7.4 is a reproduction of the model (Maldonado, 1963).

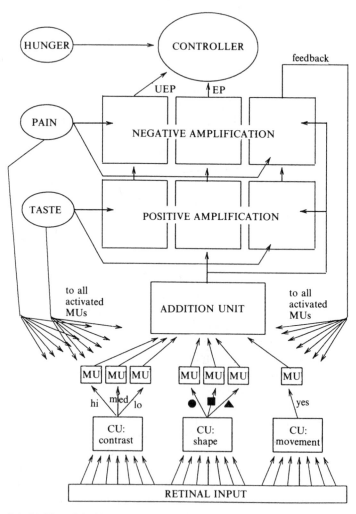

Figure 7.4 *Maldonado's block diagram model of the visual attack learning system in octopus, after Maldonado (1963): MU = memory unit; CU = classifying unit; EP = experiential parameter; UEP = unspecific effect parameter.*

The first level of processing in the model is **classifying units** (CUs), which each respond when a particular feature is present in the input: so there are CUs to recognize brightness, vertical extent, etc. Each CU is connected to several **memory units** (MUs), and there is one MU activated by each particular level of brightness which the CU output can signal; a CU recognizing shape will have MUs activated by each of the different shape signals it can output, and so on.

The visual memory of the system is stored within these MUs. Their response levels are adjusted, much like perceptron weights, upon the receipt of various reinforcement signals. So, the MU activated by a high response from the brightness CU will learn to produce a strong response if positive reinforcement arrives during its period of activation. The MU response tendencies decay in the absence of reinforcement, and it is possible that different MUs have different ranges which their response levels can assume.

In the third level of the model, an **addition unit** forms a weighted sum of all the MU responses, and this represents the strength of the decision to attack the given input. Conversely, a weak signal indicates retreat should be made. These two outputs are the only two actions which the model can learn to produce.

The attack–retreat decision travels from the addition unit, to the highest levels of the model. Here, it encounters a **two-stage amplification system**: one to amplify the positive and attack signals and one the negative and retreat signals, as shown in Figure 7.4. The output from these amplification systems, together with a parameter indicating hunger, are passed to a final controller, which sends a final attack or retreat decision out of the learning system and into the centres controlling motor output.

Reinforcement to the system is assumed to be provided by the noci-hedono receptors, which signal pain and taste experiences to the system. They pass directly to affect the response level of all activated MUs, but they also affect the operations of the amplification systems.

Each amplification system consists of three subparts. In the first, recent effects of pain and taste are combined, to produce the **unspecific effect parameter**, which contributes to a non-specific tendency to attack or retreat depending on recent reinforcement experiences. In the second, the outputs of the addition unit are simply combined to produce the **experiential parameter**, a measure of the tendency to attack or retreat based on learning in the MUs. In the third, the memory unit output together with any noci-hedono input is combined into a **feedback signal** which also travels to all activated MUs, making them slightly more likely to repeat their last outputs. This provides for the observed effect that an octopus's initial delay in attacking a novel stimulus should gradually fade with training: as the feedback levels build up in the MUs, attack should occur more quickly. It also allows a sort of short-term memory, allowing the persistence of representations of recent inputs until (potentially delayed) reinforcement arrives. Noci-hedono input, when it arrives, is applied to all *activated* MUs, so it is essential to keep recent MUs active.

Maldonado's model is meant to address possible functioning of the optic lobe – represented by CUs, MUs and addition unit – and the SFVL circuit – represented by paired amplification units and controller. The positive amplification corresponds to the superior frontal lobe, the negative amplification to the vertical lobe, and the controller to the subvertical lobe.

Maldonado's model accounts for a large portion of octopus data: it provides a delay to attack which decreases with positive learning, it incorporates the unspecific effect, and it acknowledges that visual memory should be stored in the optic lobes. It also predicts learning difficulties after ablation of the vertical lobe (corresponding to the negative amplifier), since the source of the feedback to the MUs is eliminated, and the MUs will therefore be unable to remain activated until reinforcement arrives.

There are several obvious correspondences between Maldonado's model and OVSIM. These include provision of a layer of feature-detecting cells which feed into the true memory units, reciprocal feedback with higher regions responsible for short-term memory, and existence of fairly separate mechanisms to generate the unspecific effect.

However, the two models also differ in several respects. The most basic difference is that OVSIM, based on ADB techniques, uses explicit attention-driven buffers to hold short-term memories. In Maldonado's model, short-term memories are held implicitly by maintaining the MUs in an activated state; since each MU corresponds to a perceptron weight, this approach is not unlike the eligibility trace methods of Barto, Sutton and others for delay learning (see Chapter 2). One effect of this approach is that the MUs maintained in an active state will necessarily interfere with the processing of interim images, since they will continue to output as surely as MUs activated by the new inputs instead. Yet, in octopus, the optic lobe is active in the visuomotor feedback loop which oversees locomotion and the grasping of food during the interval between attack decision and noci-hedono feedback. In OVSIM, short-term memory is implemented as a buffer distinct from the interim processing, and would therefore allow this visual feedback loop to continue.

Another difference between the models arises at the level of the feature-detecting units. In OVSIM, each responds when one of a class of patterns is present within its retinal field, and each memory unit learns the appropriate responses associated with combinations of outputs from these feature-detectors. In Maldonado's model, each MU is associated with a *single* output of each feature-detecting CU. This seems to eliminate the possibility of ever forming associations about complex features. If, for example, the system is not provided with CUs which explicitly perform 'L'-detection, it should not be possible to distinguish an 'L' except as a pattern which stimulates both horizontal and vertical edge detectors; yet the octopus can (with difficulty) learn to distinguish 'C' from 'L' shapes (Young, 1958a). Further, by this one-to-one mapping of CUs to MUs, the system is prevented from learning about correlations between CU outputs representing different features: e.g., a task of learning to attack black 'L's and white circles but not black squares. Again, this task is learnable by octopuses (Boycott and Young, 1956), and would be learnable by OVSIM as well.

There are several other smaller distinctions between the models. For example, the systems representing higher lobes in Maldonado's model serve the additional function of magnifying the current decision and feeding it back into the optic lobe; in OVSIM, the higher lobes may either perform this task, or physically implement the short-term memories themselves, although this is probably less satisfying from a biological point of view. Delay in Maldonado's model is explained as the time during which the feedback from the higher levels builds up within the MUs sufficiently to allow a decision to attack to pass threshold. In OVSIM, the delay is a direct consequence of the model's probabilistic nature, and represents the average number of cycles required to generate a high number of votes. Finally, output to the motor centres in Maldonado's model is from the controller, within the higher levels. Yet, in both the octopus and OVSIM, this output comes from the optic lobes. This is consistent with the fact that generation of appropriately learned motor outputs can continue even after ablation of the higher lobes.

However, the great attraction of Maldonado's model has been its ability to describe a wide range of complex behaviours observable in the octopus using only a handful of very simple types of element.

7.5 Conclusions

This chapter explored the plausibility of OVSIM as a high-level model of visual attack learning in octopus. That is, while the modules themselves may internally bear no resemblance to the anatomy of, for example, the optic lobe, it is possible that the ADB style of processing employed may be a good model for delay learning as accomplished by the octopus. The preliminary support for this claim comes from the previous chapter, when, in addition to being capable of learning the same kind of tasks as octopus, OVSIM showed many of the same features of learning. These included the delay to attack, the shape of the learning curve, characteristics of multiple discrimination learning, etc.

If the octopus is performing ADB in a manner similar to that done by OVSIM, then the two learning systems should degrade in the same way when the modules which perform analogous tasks are damaged in each. That was the thesis of this chapter, and it was borne out: if the vertical lobe in octopus is related to the ADB functions in OVSIM, then the deficit in learning acquisition and expression is similar when vertical lobe and ADB are disabled. This supports the idea that the octopus may be performing ADB. There are alternative models, such as Maldonado's (1963) block diagram, but the OVSIM model accounts for the data at least as well.

Now, the interesting aspect of models such as OVSIM and Maldonado's is that they can generate *predictions* which must be true in octopus if the model is accurate. This suggests a course of experiments for the biologist, and the results will either strengthen the model's claim or else show how it must be adapted or even abandoned.

There are several predictions made by OVSIM (and the ADB approach to delay learning) which it would be interesting to investigate in octopus for this reason.

First, an ADB system learns in a backward fashion. In OVSIM for example, if an attack is begun at time t, four cycles intervene before the reinforcement at time $t + 4$. In the beginning stages of training, when the attention assigned to all patterns is approximately equal, the inputs from time $t + 3$ and $t + 4$ are most likely to occupy the two-element buffer. These must be associated with the reinforcement, and the response to them must drop on subsequent trials, before their attention also drops. Only then do patterns $t + 2$, $t + 1$ and eventually t come to occupy the buffer when reinforcement arrives. Therefore, in the intermediate stages of learning, the system will give a higher response to the inputs from time $t + 4$ and $t + 3$ than to the true stimulus t. If the octopus uses a similar strategy to ADB, then it must correspondingly be the case that at some point the animal will have a higher tendency to attack visual images corresponding to $t + 4$ and $t + 3$ (if these can be constructed) than to the true stimulus image t.

This might be difficult to investigate, because it may be hard to 'construct' intervening images corresponding to $t + 3$ and $t + 4$ in OVSIM. At the very least, it might involve darkening the room while one of the octopus's arms was moved into position. This manipulation might in itself have enough impact on the octopus to influence learning rates or other behaviour.

A second prediction reflects the fact that OVSIM buffers input based on the unpredictability of reinforcement to each. Therefore, the probability that the pattern from time t is still in the buffer at time $t + 4$ depends critically on the predictability of the intervening patterns. In the OVSIM simulations discussed here, the intervening patterns are constant for any one stimulus pattern. But this is not necessary: it would be equally possible to fill the intervening cycles with random input patterns. In this case, if the intervening patterns were purely novel and purely unpredictable, pattern t would *never* remain in the buffer long enough to be associated with the reinforcement at time $t + 4$. If the intervening patterns are wholly predictable, pattern t may be able to remain buffered until reinforcement on the trial of its first showing. So, the time to learn t depends on the predictability of intervening stimuli. In octopus, the implication is that if the visual input were disrupted in the interval between attack decision and reinforcement, the buffering would similarly be disrupted, and learning time would be affected accordingly. This would be easier to carry out experimentally.

Young (1958a) has noted that it is possible to explain the effects of vertical lobe ablation simply in terms of domination of UE^+ after elimination of the UE^- mechanism. The most obvious effect of vertical lobe ablation is an increase in the non-specific level of attack. However, Young (1958a) found that if positive reinforcement was withheld during trials with ablated octopus, and thus UE^+ was kept low, performance improved. This implies that the animals could learn the discrimination, but could not express their learning in the presence of so strong a UE^-. In OVSIM, the corresponding deficit includes, but is not limited to, elimination of UE^-. It also very definitely includes damage to short-term memory maintenance. Accordingly, the OVSIM model predicts that vertical lobe ablation should show this. For example, the ablated octopus should be unable to perform any task involving short-term memory. Such a task might involve showing a white square *followed by* a crab as a positive stimulus, and a black square followed by a crab as the negative one. To solve this task, the animal would have to maintain information about earlier inputs. If a normal animal can learn to execute this task, then the OVSIM model predicts its performance will be severely disrupted after removal of the vertical lobe; certainly a R–T animal should be unable to learn to perform this.

A final interesting point, although not strictly a prediction, raised by considering OVSIM as a model of visual attack learning in octopus, concerns the issue of the indivisibility of attack. In OVSIM, once the system generates an attack output, the next four cycles are pre-determined: there is no way in which the system can 'change its mind' and recall the output. This is obviously a simplification which could be refined in later versions of the simulation, and it is certainly the case that an octopus can be observed to approach and retreat without touching the stimulus, or to gingerly put its arm around a crab, trying not to touch the nearby negative square (Boycott and Young, 1955). At the same time, there are a few data indicating that once the animal has definitely made a decision to attack, it cannot stop it. For example, if an octopus begins an attack and the lights in the experimental room are then extinguished, the animal carries through the attack regardless (Muntz and Gwyther, 1988). An even more suggestive effect is observed in animals which have been trained to discriminate vertical from horizontal sinusoidal gratings of varying frequency. If the animal is trained to attack only vertical gratings, and is then shown a horizontal pattern which is too fine to be distinguished at a distance, the animal eventually attacks (Muntz and Gwyther, 1988). Yet, as the animal approaches in the course of the attack, it may be able to make out the stripe pattern and realise its error. Despite this, the animal completes the attack. This certainly suggests that once the animal has decided to attack, the action is unstoppable. If this really is the case, then it lessens the need for delay-bridging mechanisms such as ADB, since the animal can simply hold the single image to which the attack responds. However, such a system seems to contradict the known involvement of the optic lobe in ongoing visuomotor feedback loops (Young, 1964). It would be self-defeating for such a system to be disabled during attack – surely when visual feedback for the fine-tuning of motor output is most required. This phenomenon is certainly important enough to warrant further investigation.

8

ADB and delay learning in higher animals

The attention-driven buffering concept was devised in order to answer the following three basic criteria.

- Learning should be **exploratory**: reinforcements and, to some degree, subsequent inputs should be dependent on the system's own outputs. In operant conditioning, for example, reinforcement is defined to be contingent on the exhibition of some response by the animal. Exploratory learning is in contrast to much of artificial network learning in which the input and output are often selected by algorithm or by the trainer during learning stages.

- **Reinforcement learning** is required: the reinforcement to the system may only take the form of a global scalar – often conveniently thought of as indicating the 'success' or 'appropriateness' of the system's output. This is in contrast, in ANN research, to supervised learning which provides the desired outputs and unsupervised learning, which provides no external reinforcement.

- Learning should be able to cope with the complication that the reinforcement signal may not follow immediately after the response which elicits it; during the delay, reinforcement from other responses may well arrive and intervene. Therefore, the system must perform **delay learning**. In ANN research, the reinforcement generally arrives immediately after some output is produced, and well before the arrival of the next input requiring response.

The ADB system satifies these criteria: both theoretically, as shown in the examples of Chapter 5, and also in a more realistic context such as the operant conditioning tasks of Chapter 6. It could be quite fairly argued, however, that this has very little bearing on the solution of more advanced forms of learning problems by the brains of higher animals, such as mammals and even primates. Even if OVSIM, for example, provided an absolutely accurate model of operant conditioning in the octopus, the cephalopod and vertebrate brains are different enough that there is little reason to assume that the organizing principles of one should hold true in the other. Therefore, there is no defensible assumption that solving the secrets of the octopus brain leaves us any closer to understand how mammalian brains perform operant conditioning. And, even if it did, the argument continues, understanding how mammalian brains perform operant conditioning does not necessarily imply an understanding of how the most interesting learning problems are solved. These include the very highest level functions, such as for example credit assignment, rule-formation, and construction of models of others' behaviour.

This argument involves two basic questions. The first is whether higher animals perform anything usefully comparable to the operations performed by ADB; the second is whether there is any suggestion that they perform these operations in a manner related to attention-driven buffering.

8.1 Physiological relevance of ADB objectives

For ADB to be relevant to animal learning, it must first be shown that animals perform under the same criteria specified above: namely exploratory learning, reinforcement learning, and delay learning. This does not require that *all* instances of learning satisfy these same criteria, only that enough do to require that the animal needs to be able to learn under these conditions.

In its strictest sense, exploratory learning is in contrast to **passive learning**. In turn, a passive learning system has a discrete learn phase, during which the environment or some teacher generates input and output which the system learns to associate. This learn phase is necessarily separate from the operate phase, in which, given an input, the system reproduces (as best it can) the associated output. So, in passive learning, knowledge acquisition is dissociated from knowledge retrieval or use.

The dissociation of knowledge acquisition from knowledge retrieval is completely at odds with the biological advantage given to an animal which is capable of learning. The advantage of being able to learn is that an animal can adapt to new or changing environments. An animal with first a 'learn' phase and then a subsequent 'operate' phase would have no survival advantage over an animal which simply had all of these behaviours genetically pre-wired as instinctive behaviours. In fact, this seems never to be the case, as all animals tested so far can at least habituate – learning to stop responding to stimuli which repeatedly prove irrelevant (Wells, 1968) – and therefore can learn to adapt their behaviour to at least some of the features of their environment.

The existence of passive learning is a controversial issue in psychology. For example, when a school child memorizes associations such as embodied in a multiplication table, is she simply learning that an input (7 times 7) should produce an output (49) – or is there much more complex memory formation going on? There have certainly been documented instances of learning by observation: as described in Chapter 1, children shown movies of adults attacking a doll and then being rewarded with sweets are later more likely to show unprompted aggressive behaviour towards the doll than are children seeing a movie in which attacks were punished by scolding (Fisher, 1980). The behaviour in this case resembles passive learning in that the subject comes to produce a response to a stimulus without any prior behaviour pairing that stimulus and response.

However, it is not at all clear that this is the same phenomenon as passive learning in an ANN. At the very least, there is probably complex memory reorganization during learning which the ANN definition of passive learning would disallow. For example, the child may watch the movie, imagine or simulate the relative advantage of obtaining sweets, and test a hypothesis that by mimicking the behaviour in the movie a sweet may be obtained. If this description is accurate, the child is still displaying exploratory learning in the form of hypothesis testing.

There are also convincing experiments that, if the exploratory nature of learning is suppressed, animals learn less well or not at all. A classic example is **learned helplessness**. In a learned helplessness experiment, the animal is prevented from doing anything to influence the arrival of reinforcement, but might observe another animal making the correct response; usually the animal is not able to learn by observation. An example experiment (described in Pearce, 1987) contained three classes of dogs A, B, and C, each held in a hammock. The dogs in group A were occasionally given electric shocks; those in B were also shocked, but could turn off the shock by pressing a panel with their noses. Group C dogs were not shocked at all. In the second phase of the experiment, the dogs were placed into avoidance chambers. Here, the sounding of a tone warned that shock would follow within a few seconds, but the dogs could prevent this by moving to the far end of the chamber. Group B and C dogs could quickly learn to avoid shock. Group A dogs were unable to learn to prevent the shock; further, they were even unable to learn to move to the far end of the chamber to escape from the shock. One interpretation of this kind of result it that it is the lack of effectiveness of any response during the earlier phase which inhibits the animals' later learning of an operant response (Pearce, 1987).

The debate continues. However, it seems unlikely that passive learning is very descriptive of any animal learning. As Hunter (1988) concludes: "Learning, loosely stated, is the improvement of an organism's ability to achieve its goals on the basis of its experience. Clamping the input and output of the system to a desired state [ANN passive learning] is not what is traditionally meant by experience".

Reinforcement learning is likewise much more prominent in animal learning than supervised learning. Supervised learning requires the provision of the desired output by an external teacher; the system's role is to learn to reproduce the desired output given a particular input. To some extent, this can be found in human learning. Again, the memorization of a multiplication table involves the student learning to produce the correct output (a product) given two inputs (the multiplicands). In humans and other animals which parent their young, there is also a form of learning which can roughly be classified as supervised: imitation. The young watch the response of the parent to given stimuli, and perhaps the response of the parent can be taken to represent the desired output. Even so, this is at best a metaphor for supervised learning: the basic shape of the response is specified, but the details are not.

For example, in the learning of a motor response to a sensory stimulus, which is a very basic and ubiquitous form of learning, a teacher would have to predict 'how each motoneuron involved in the task should respond to each afferent volley, and would have to be able to provide these motoneurons with this information.... it is hard to imagine where such detailed information could come from.' (Barto, 1987).

The other alternative to reinforcement learning is **unsupervised learning**. This certainly does occur in animal learning, within the primary sensory cortices. For example, human primary visual cortex self-organizes during the first months of life so that various regions respond maximally to various visual features present in the environment. This is an important technique; but because self-organizing systems by definition do not make use of external reinforcement signals, they alone are not sufficient to produce the kind of response learning evident in conditioning, habituation, sensitization, and even higher forms of learning.

Therefore, reinforcement learning must also occur within animals.

Finally, there has already been extensive argument in earlier chapters that delay learning is a common phenomenon in animal learning. It was shown in Chapter 6 that even invertebrates such as the octopus can be conditioned when the delay between decision to act and arrival of reinforcement may take seconds. There is also a body of literature documenting delay learning experiments with higher animals. Some were mentioned previously: learning to avoid food when ingestion was followed with irradiation to produce nausea (Walker, 1987), or to prefer food when ingestion was followed by vitamin injections (Garcia *et al.*, 1967), and so on. Even if these reinforcers are delayed by several hours, the animal learns to seek or avoid the food which, it believes, causes the after-effects (Feldman, 1981). In humans, the delay between action and reinforcement can last for days and longer. It is therefore apparent that all of these animals have mechanisms allowing them to perform delay learning.

8.2 Possible methods

Given that animal learning involves exploratory, reinforcement and delay learning, the next question to consider is how animals might accomplish these tasks, and whether their methods can be said to bear any similarity to ADB.

It is accepted that animals have some form of short-term memory (or even intermediate-term memory) as this is how the gap until delayed reinforcement arrives must be bridged. In human beings, STM is often thought of as taking the form of a limited-size buffer, with capacity for some 5–7 items at once – this being the maximum number of terms a person can remember at once, if allowed uninterrupted rehearsal of the items. However, once rehearsal is interrupted, items in STM have a half-life of some 10–15 seconds before they are lost (Johnson-Laird, 1982). ADB also involves a limited-capacity buffer, in which items are lost when new, higher-attention items intervene.

There is increasing evidence that the view of STM as holding 'seven plus or minus two' items is oversimplified. These items can be individual letters, whole words, or even sentences. It is possible that there is a short-term store for each kind of information. Baddely and Hitch conclude that STM must therefore contain at least three components: a central executive, a short-term visuo-spatial store, and a short-term speech store (Johnson-Laird, 1982). The speech store can be rehearsed and therefore has a maximum capacity of as much information as can be verbally rehearsed within some three seconds. The visual store cannot be rehearsed verbally, and therefore is limited to contain some 2–3 items.

The ADB systems defined in this book can associate a part of the buffer with every memory unit. If different cells in the memory are associated with strongly differing information types, then there would effectively be the possibility of buffering several instances of each information type.

In humans, at least, it seems that rehearsal of items makes them more likely to enter long-term memory or to be retrievable from long-term memory (Carlson, 1986). In ADB, as in many ANN models involving short-term memory (c.f. Grossberg, 1971), items in STM have correlates in LTM which are strengthened with each cycle that the information remains in the buffer and reinforcement is present. This sort of approach requires an STM mechanism which maintains activity in relevant cells for a reasonably long period of time. One way in which this might be achieved is by reverberation: a cycle of cells which activate each other to form a circuit which may remain active until something occurs to interrupt the sequence.

In fact, reverberating circuits have been found in the small nervous systems of some invertebrates such as lobster (Selverston, 1988), typically governing central pattern generation such as might be needed to produce a rhythmic heartbeat.

In mammalian cortex, such reverberation may also exist. In clinically isolated but intact cortical regions, containing cells which are normally quiet, a train of electric pulses can cause bursts of activity across the region which might continue as long as thirty minutes (Carlson, 1986); a single large shock to the centre of the region can then stop all activity. The suggestion is that the region was reverberating, once started by the initial pulses; the larger burst caused all the neurons to fire at once. Immediately after a neuron fires, there is a short refractory period during which it cannot fire again. If all neurons in the region fire at once, all will then simultaneously enter the refractory period, and reverberation will be silenced.

This does not prove, of course, that such reverberation actually occurs in intact cortex, or that it is actually the mechanism which sustains short-term memory. However, events which interrupt electrical activity in the brain, such as blows to the head, electroconvulsive therapy, and epilepsy, also have disruptive effects on short-term memory (Stein, 1987). This supports the theory that reverberations have been interrupted, causing loss of information which was held in STM.

It thus appears that animals would be capable of maintaining an STM buffer like that required for ADB. They would also need to be capable of executing the attention-assigning function which governs which elements occupy that buffer.

The probability of an item entering the ADB buffer in the first place is related to its attention, which is a measure of how 'unpredictable' the item is. This concept of learning being based on a need to resolve unpredictable events is extant in psychological theory. Notably, Kelly's Personal Construct Theory suggests that an animal (or human) has as its chief motivation the desire to resolve ambiguities in its input – and to be able to predict results and anticipate its own next input (Kelly, 1955). Animals have shown that they do 'learn for learning's sake' even when there is no other ostensible motivation than curiosity. For example, rats turned loose in a maze will explore, and can later return efficiently to where they saw food when they were not hungry (Walker, 1987).

Such a curiosity-driven theory of learning entails that the animal must be able to recognize these ambiguities when they arise. This means that the animal must have the ability to judge unpredictability, like is provided by the attention-assigning component of an ADB system. It is worth emphasizing that this requires not merely a novelty detector, but one which measures a stimulus's unpredictability – a stimulus may be familiar but still ambiguous. As will be discussed below, this is a putative role for the amygdala in mammals.

Another implication of the ADB system is that the buffer is separate from the cells or portion of the cells which perform the ongoing processing and which actually maintain LTM. The alternative, that the same cells maintain STM and LTM, raises the problem of processing information while STM is being held. Further, as Grossberg (1987) notes: if only unpredictable events enter STM, how is it that very predictable stimuli can still be processed? A straightforward solution is to separate STM from LTM and processing.

As it happens, the idea of keeping STM in a buffer separate from LTM and from ongoing processing is not incompatible with physiological data. The popular current hypothesis of memory formation involves long-term potentiation (LTP), which is defined as a long-lasting increase in synaptic efficacy produced by high-frequency stimulation of afferents (Berger, 1984); its counterpart, long-term depression, can produce a decrease in efficacy (Stanton and Sejnowski, 1989). LTP mechanisms are still a topic of research, but there are several theories which posit a change which does not participate in the short-term operation of the neuronal circuit (Lynch and Baudry, 1984). This would allow short- and long-term processing to co-exist in the cell with minimal mutual interference.

A final major implication of the ADB system which must be reconciled with physiological data is its prediction of backward conditioning. In normal classical conditioning, an unconditioned stimulus (UCS) is chosen which reliably elicits a response (R). Then if a conditioned stimulus (CS) is repeatedly presented just before the UCS, it will eventually come to elicit R even if the UCS is no longer presented. Eventually, if the CS is repeatedly presented without the UCS, it ceases to elicit the response R.

For maximum effect, the CS should be presented some fixed time before the UCS. The actual optimal timing is dependent both on the species being trained and also on the response being tested. If the delay is much longer than this optimum, the CS is irrelevant; if the delay is less, the CS has no value as a predictor of the UCS and will not be learned (Klopf, 1986). If the UCS onset actually precedes CS onset, a set-up termed backward conditioning, the CS may actually come to inhibit the elicitation of R (Klopf, 1986), although the effects may be quite complex.

However, backward operant conditioning can actually result in formation of associations. Hudson (Walker, 1987) electrified a food cup with a striped pattern; after a week the rats no longer ate from the cup but piled sawdust over it as if to hide the pattern and retreated. If the experimental setup was changed so that as the shock was administered, the lights went out and the cup was removed, many of the rats failed to learn the association. This implies that the association was formed in the period immediately following reinforcement administration. Hudson also found that if pipe cleaners were dropped into the cage just after the shock, the rats would selectively avoid those (Walker, 1987). Similarly, Keith-Lucas and Guttman introduced a toy animal into the cage within seconds after the shock, and found that the rats would develop a conditioned aversion to the toy (Walker, 1987). All of these experiments indicate that the few seconds immediately following the US are critical to the formation of associations.

The ADB system will associate reinforcement with whatever is currently in its buffer. If the items have high attention, they will be reinforced and items occurring just after the UCS but unable to enter the buffer will be ignored. If those new items can get into the buffer, the reinforcement will be attributed to them, and backward conditioning will occur. This is one explanation consistent with the above effects in animals.

8.3 Possible mechanisms for ADB

Finally, it is worth a short consideration of where the ADB operations might possibly occur within the mammalian brain. The hippocampus, amygdala,

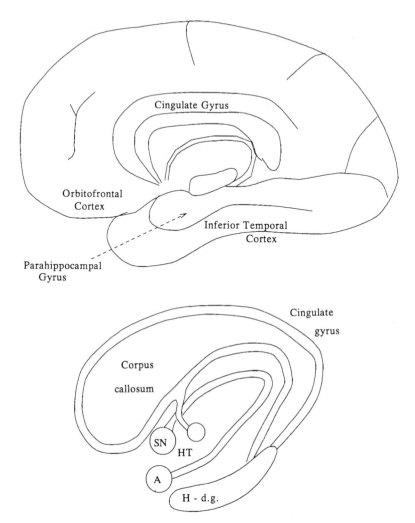

Figure 8.1 *Top: medial view of human brain, showing some regions involved in memory formation. Bottom: deeper exposure of temporal lobe, showing more implicated regions. SN = septal nucleus; HT = hypothalamus; A = amygdala; H-d.g. = hippocampal/ dentate gyrus complex.*

hypothalamus, orbitofrontal cortex, and inferior temporal cortex are all highly interconnected in mammals, and all seem to be implicated in learning responses to reinforcement, but not in producing those responses once learned. This makes them good candidates for involvement in STM processing which is separate from LTM processing.

There is a huge body of literature documenting impairments which appear after lesion of these regions – in particular the hippocampal system, which includes hippocampus, dentate gyrus, entorhinal cortex, and the major efferents and afferents to these structures. In humans, damage to hippocampus and associated cortex produces severe retrograde amnesia, resulting in an inability to learn new declarative facts, but little or no disruption of knowledge acquired before the trauma. Procedural or skill learning is often still possible in these patients, although they may be unable to remember their training sessions (Squire, 1987). The data are extensive and often conflict between and even within species, and give rise to several theories of the function of this part of the brain. An important theory based on human data is that the hippocampal system is necessary for acquisition of declarative, or factual, knowledge while other brain systems are responsible for procedural learning (Squire, 1987). Other theories, derived from learning impairments observed in ahippocampal animals, suggest a primary role in cognitive mapping (O'Keefe and Nadel, 1978), configural learning (Sutherland and Rudy, 1989), and learning where there is a delay between stimulus and response or reinforcement (Olton, 1983). Particularly this last idea has a clear relationship to ADB.

Involvement in short- and intermediate-term memory has been suggested to be the chief role of the hippocampus (Rawlins, 1985; Olton, 1983), although such an account does not address why ahippocampal animals should be impaired at spatial learning which has no temporal component (e.g., Eichenbaum, et al., 1990). Even if this is an incomplete account, there is certainly a role for the hippocampal system in delay learning. Ahippocampal animals cannot perform trace conditioning, where the CS terminates some time before the UCS, and the animal must maintain a memory or trace of the CS during the interval (Moyer, et al., 1990). Another classic impairment in animals with damage to these regions is delayed non-match to sample: where the animal must choose objects which were not rewarded on previous presentations (Gaffan, 1983). Hippocampal damage in humans results in somewhat analogous deficits. The patients have intact short-term memory and can remember items indefinitely if allowed to repeat them or otherwise rehearse; but once their attention is turned to something else, the information will be lost (Squire, 1987).

Neurophysiological evidence also implicates this region in short- or intermediate-term memory. In fact, recent recordings show that activity in the dentate gyrus, part of the hippocampal formation, maintains a trace of recent auditory inputs during an auditory classification task (Deadwyler, 1985). The pattern of connectivity within certain regions of the hippocampus seems to lend itself to autoassociation – in much the same way as highly interconnected artificial neural networks are useful for this task. Such systems can store and retrieve patterns of input activity for a short period of time, until overwritten by new inputs. Many computational models of hippocampus have stressed this capability for autoassociation, which might have various roles when embedded within a larger system (McNaughton and Morris, 1987, and

Rolls, 1989). If regions of hippocampus do function as autoassociators, then they would certainly be capable of serving as a buffer for ADB operations–maintaining a selection of recent events for a short period of time until reinforcement arrives. This would not interfere with other operations which might occur within the hippocampal region, and indeed such a function seems to be suggested by many of the data mentioned above.

A second interesting aspect of the hippocampal system is that it seems to be involved in novelty detection. Cells have been found within inferomedial temporal cortex which fire more strongly on first presentation of a stimulus than on subsequent presentations (Brown, et al., 1987). At a behavioral level, combined lesions of hippocampus and amygdala in monkey result in impairments at novelty-matching (Mishkin, 1978) and delay-matching (Zola-Morgan, et al., 1982). Hippocampal cells have also been found which fire when the animal is in a.particular situation or location and does not find what it expects there (O'Keefe, 1979). Such measures of novelty and unexpectedness are two strongly appropriate factors from which a measure of attention might be derived within ADB.

Thus, both of the critical mechanisms of ADB, that of a separate short-term buffer and of attention-assigning capability, have possible substrates within the mammalian brain. There is a strong case that they could be carried out within the hippocampal formation, which does not conflict with the idea that the hippocampus's role may be much more extensive.

Obviously, the story of learning in mammalian brains is enormously complicated. If ADB has any accuracy in modelling mammalian learning, it is only a tiny portion of the story. But delay learning is an important aspect of learning nonetheless, from the human being down to the lowly octopus and beyond.

Probably the most intriguing aspect of this work has been that a system which was originally developed from purely pragmatic machine learning specifications should turn out to have some similarities to the solution found by nature in the octopus to the problem of delay learning. If it were to turn out that these similarities hold in any detail in higher brains as well, there would be a rather dramatic conclusion to be drawn: that there may actually be only one fairly constrained way in which to accomplish this learning. On the other hand, if these parallels are eventually shown to be misleading, then the opposite conclusion holds, and there may in fact be many different ways in which to construct an 'intelligent' learning machine.

This an intriguing question. But it seems clear that the approach to answering it must continue on two fronts: the bottom-up approach, whereby physiologists and psychologists continue to provide data on how brains accomplish their tasks, and the top-down approach, in which engineers and cognitive scientists propose models to satisfy these data and to make predictions which discriminate between these models. From this point of view, it is just as important to discover which models of learning are *not* satisfactory – and why – as this will still provide valuable information. Whether ADB has any validity or not as a psychological model, therefore, examination of it and similar models, and testing of the predictions they raise, can still contribute at least some small clues as to how intelligent learning systems can one day be constructed.

References

Ackley, D. and Littman, M. (1990) Learning from natural selection in an artificial environment. *Proc. International Joint Conference on Neural Networks*, Washington, I, 189–93.

Al-Alawi, R. and Stonham, T. (1990) Evaluation of the functional capacities of multilayered logical neural networks. *Proc. INNC-90-PARIS*, Paris, p. 983 (abstract only).

Aleksander, I. and Stonham, T. (1979) Guide to pattern recognition using random-access memories. *IEE J. Computers and Digital Techniques*, 2(1), 29–40.

Aleksander, I., Thomas, W. and Bowden, P. (1984) WISARD – A radical step forward in image recognition. *Sensor Review*, 4(3), 120–4.

Aleksander, I. and Wilson, M. (1985) Adaptive windows for image processing. *IEE Proceedings*, 132E(5), 233–45.

Aleksander, I. (1988) Logical connectionist systems, in *Neural Computers* (Eds. R. Eckmiller, C. von der Malsburg), Springer-Verlag, Berlin, pp. 189–97.

Aleksander, I. (1989) Canonical nets based on logic nodes. *Proc. 1st IEE International Conference on Artificial Neural Networks*, London, 110–14.

Aleksander, I. (1990) Ideal neurons for neural computers, in *Parallel Processing in Neural Systems and Computers* (Eds. R. Eckmiller, G. Hartmann, G. Hauske), Elsevier Science, Amsterdam, pp. 161–4.

Aleksander, I. and Morton, H. (1990) *An Introduction to Neural Computing*, Chapman and Hall, London.

Barto, A. and Sutton, R. (1981) Landmark learning-: an illustration of associative search. *Biological Cybernetics* 42, 1–8.

Barto, A., Sutton, R. and Brouwer, P. (1981) Associative search network: a reinforcement learning associative memory. *Biological Cybernetics*, 40, 201–11.

Barto, A. and Sutton, R. (1982) Simulation of anticipatory responses in classical conditioning by a neuron-like adaptive element. *Behavioural Brain Research*, 4, 221–35.

Barto, A., Sutton, R. and Anderson, C. (1983) Neuronlike adaptive elements that can solve difficult learning control problems. *IEEE Trans. on Systems, Man and Cybernetics*, SMC-13(5), 834–51.

Barto, A. (1987) An approach to learning control surfaces by connectionist systems, in *Vision, Brain and Cooperative Competition* (Eds. M. Arbib, A. Hanson), MIT Press, London, pp. 665–701.

Berger, T. (1984) Long-term potentiation of hippocampal synaptic transmission affects rate of behavioral learning. *Science*, 224, 627–30.

Blakemore, C. (1975) Central visual processing, in *Handbook of Physiology* (Eds. M. Gazzaniga, C. Blakemore), Academic Press, London, pp. 241–68.

Blakemore, C. (1988) *The Mind Machine*, BBC Books, London.

Bledsoe, W. and Browning, I. (1959) Pattern recognition and reading by machine. *Proc. Eastern Joint Computer Conference*, Boston, pp. 225–32.

Boycott, B. and Young, J. Z. (1955) A memory system in Octopus vulgaris Lamarck. *Proc. Royal Society of London*, **B143**, 449–80.

Boycott, B. and Young, J. Z. (1956) Effects of interference with the vertical lobe on visual discrimination in Octopus vulgaris Lamarck. *Proc. Royal Society of London*, **B146**, 439–59.

Boycott, B. (1967) Learning in the octopus, in *Psychobiology, The Biological Basis of Behavior* (Eds. J. McGaugh, N. Weinberger, R. Whalen), W.H. Freeman, San Francisco, pp. 132–40.

Brown, M., Wilson, F. and Riches, I. (1987) Neuronal evidence that inferomedial temporal cortex is more important than hippocampus in certain processes underlying recognition memory. *Brain Research*, **409**, 158–62.

Carlson, N. (1986) *The Physiology of Behavior*, Allyn and Bacon, London.

Carnevalli, P. and Patarnello, S. (1987) Exhaustive thermodynamical analysis of boolean learning networks. *Europhysics Letters*, **4**(10), 1199–1204.

Carpenter, G. and Grossberg, S. (1988) The ART of adaptive pattern recognition by a self-organising network. *IEEE Computer*, **21**(3), 77–88.

Cecconi, F. and Parisi, D. (1989) Networks that learn to predict where the food is and also to eat it. *Proc. IJCNN-89, Washington*, **2**, p. 624 (abstract only).

Clarkson, T., Gorse, D. and Taylor, J. (1989) Hardware realisable models of neural processing. *Proc. 1st IEE International Conference on Artificial Neural Networks*, London, 242–6.

Clarkson, T., Gorse, D. and Taylor, J. (1991) A serial-update VLSI architecture for the learning probabilistic RAM neuron, in *Artificial Neural Networks* (Eds. T. Kohonen, et al.), Elsevier Science, North Holland, pp. 1573–6.

Deadwyler, S. (1985) A physiological basis for hippocampal involvement in coding temporally discontiguous events. *Behavioral and Brain Sciences*, **8**(3), 500–501.

Doran, J. (1968) Experiments with a pleasure-seeking automation, in *Machine Intelligence* (Ed. D. Mitchie), Edinburgh University Press, Edinburgh, **3**, pp. 195–216.

Durbin, R. and Rumelhart, D. (1989) Product units: A computationally powerful and biologically plausible extension to backpropagation networks. *Neural Computation*, **1**, 133–42.

Eichenbaum, H., Stewart, C. and Morris, R. (1990) Hippocampal representation in place learning. *Journal of Neuroscience*, **10**(11), 3531–42.

Eysenck, M. (1984) *A Handbook of Cognitive Psychology*, Lawrence Erlbaum, London.

Feldman, J. (1981) A connectionist model of visual memory, in *Parallel Models of Associative Memory* (Eds. G. Hinton, J. Anderson), Lawrence Erlbaum, Hillsdale, NJ, pp. 49–81.

Filho, E., Bisset, D. and Fairhurst, M. (1990) A goal seeking neuron for boolean neural networks. *Proc. INNC-90-PARIS*, Paris, **2**, 894–7.

Fisher, Harry (1980) Three accounts of human development, in *A Handbook of Psychology* (Eds. J. Radford, E. Gover), Sheldon Press, London, pp. 449–69.

Fulcher, E. (1991) WIS-ART: Unsupervised clustering with RAM discriminators.

Neural Systems Engineering Group Internal Report NSEIR/EPF#4/91, Imperial College, Dept. Elec. Eng.

Gaffan, D. (1983) Animal amnesia: Some disconnection syndromes? in *Neurobiology of the Hippocampus* (Ed. W. Seifert), Academic Press, London, 513–28.

Garcia, J., Ervin, F., Yorke, C. and Koelling, R. (1967) Conditioning with vitamin injections. *Science*, **185**, 824–31.

Gluck, M. and Bower, G. (1988) Evaluating an adaptive network model of human learning. *J. of Memory and Language*, **27**, 166–95.

Gorse, D. and Taylor, J. (1988) On the equivalence and properties of noisy neural and probabilistic RAM nets. *Physics Letters A*, **131**(6), 326–32.

Gorse, D. (1989) A new model of the neuron, in *New Developments in Neural Computing* (Eds. J. Taylor, C. Mannion), Adam Hilger, Bristol, pp.79–86.

Gorse, D. and Taylor, J. (1990) Training strategies for probabilistic RAMs, in *Parallel Processing in Neural Systems and Computers* (Eds. R. Eckmiller, G. Hartmann, G. Hauske), Elsevier Science, Amsterdam, pp. 161–4.

Grossberg, S. (1971) On the dynamics of operant conditioning. *J. of Theoretical Biology*, **33**, 225–55.

Grossberg, S. (1980) How does a brain build cognitive code? *Psychological Review*, **87**, 1–51.

Grossberg, S. (1987) *The Adaptive Brain*, Elsevier Science, New York.

Hartwick, E., Ambrose, R. and Robinson, S. (1984) Den utilization and the movements of tagged O. dofleini. *Marine Behavior and Physiology*, **11**(2), 95–110.

Hubel, D. and Wiesel, T. (1968) Receptive fields and functional architecture in two nonstriate visual areas (18 and 19) of the cat. *J. Neurophysiology*, **28**, 229–89.

Hubel, D. and Wiesel, T. (1968) Receptive fields and functional architecture of monkey striate cortex. *J. Physiology*, **195**, 215–43.

Hunter, L. (1988) Some memory but no mind. *Behavioral and Brain Sciences*, **11**(1), 37.

Johnson-Laird, P. (1982) *The Computer and the Mind*, Fontana Paperbacks, London.

Kan, W.-K. and Aleksander, I. (1987) A probabilistic logic neuron network for associative learning. *Proc. IEEE 1st Annual International Conference on Neural Networks*, San Diego, pp. 541–8.

Kan, W. (1988) A probabilistic logic neural network for associative learning. Unpublished PhD Thesis, Imperial College, University of London.

Kelly, G. (1955) *The Theory of Personal Constructs*, Norton, New York.

Klopf, A. (1986) A drive-reinforcement model of single neuron function: an alternative to the Hebbian model, in *Neural Network for Computing* (Ed. J. Denker), American Institute of Physics, New York, pp. 265–70.

Klopf, A. (1988) A neuronal model of classical conditioning. *Psychobiology*, **16**(2), 85–125.

Kohonen, T. (1984) *Self-Organization and Associative Memory*, Springer-Verlag, New York.

Kohonen, T. (1988) The "neural" phonetic typewriter. *Computer*, **21**(3), 11–22.

Kuperstein, M. and Rubenstein, J. (1989) Implementation of an adaptive neural controller for sensory-motor coordination. *Proc. International Joint Conference on Neural Networks*, Washington, **II**, 305–10.

LeCun, Y. (1986) Learning processes in an asymmetric threshold network, in *Disordered Systems and Biological Organization* (Eds. E. Bienenstock, F. Fogelman Souli, G. Weisbuch), Springer-Verlag, Berlin.

Lettvin, J., Maturana, H., McCulloch, W. and Pitts, W. (1965) What the frog's eye tells the frog's brain, in *Embodiments of Mind* (Ed. W. McCulloch), MIT Press, Cambridge, pp.230–55.

Lucy, J. (1991) Perfect auto-associators using RAM-type nodes. *Electronics Letters*, **27**(10), 799–800.

Lynch, G. and Baudry, M. (1984) The biochemistry of memory: a new specific hypothesis. *Science*, **224**, 1057–63.

Maldonado, H. (1963) The visual attack learning system in Octopus vulgaris. *J. Theoretical Biology*, **5**, 470–88.

Martland, D. (1988) Adaptation of boolean networks using back-error propagation. (Preprint obtained from author.)

Mather, J. (1982) Factors affecting the spatial distribution of natural populations of O. joubini Robson. *Animal Behaviour*, **30**(4), 1166–70.

Mather, J. (1985) Behavioral interactions and activity of captive Eledone moschata: laboratory investigations of a "social" octopus. *Animal Behavior*, **33**(4), 1138–44.

Maturana, H. and Frenk, S. (1963) Directional movement and horizontal edge detectors in the pigeon retina. *Science*, **142**, 977–89.

McCulloch, W. and Pitts, W. (1943) A logical calculus of the ideas immanent in nervous activity. *Bulletin of Mathematical Biophysics*, **5**, 115–33.

McNaughton, B. and Morris, R. (1987) Hippocampal synaptic enhancement and information storage within a distributed memory system. *Trends in Neuroscience*, **10**(10), 408–15.

Mel, B. (1988) MURPHY: A robot that learns by doing, in *Neural Information Processing Systems* (Ed. D. Anderson), American Institute of Physics, New York, pp. 543–53.

Miller, G. (1956) The magical number seven, plus or minus two: Some limits on our capacity for processing information. *Psychological Review*, **63**, 81–97.

Mishkin, M. (1978) Memory in monkeys severely impaired by combined but not by separate removal of amygdala and hippocampus. *Nature*, **273**, 297–9.

Mitchie, D. and Chambers, R. (1968) BOXES: An experiment in adaptive control, in *Machine Intelligence 2* (Eds. E. Dale, D. Mitchie), Oliver and Boyd, Edinburgh, pp. 137–52.

Morasso, P. (1989) Neural models of cursive script handwriting. *Proc. IJCNN-90, Washington*, **2**, 539–42.

Moser, M. and Smolensky, P. (1989) Using relevance to reduce network size automatically. *Connection Science*, **1** (1), 3–16.

Moyer, J., Deyo, R. and Disterhoff, J. (1990) Hippocampectomy disrupts trace eye-blink conditioning in rabbits. *Behavioral Neuroscience*, **104** (2), 243–52.

Muntz, W. and Gwyther, J. (1988) Visual acuity in Octopus pallidus and Octopus australis. *J. Experimental Biology*, **134**, 119–29.

Myers, C. and Aleksander, I. (1988) Learning algorithms for probabilistic logic nodes. *Abstracts of 1st Annual INNS Meeting*, Boston, p.205 (abstract only).

Myers, C. (1989) Output functions for probabilistic logic nodes. *Proc. 1st IEE International Conference on Artifical Neural Networks, London*, pp. 310–14.

Myers, C. (1990) Reinforcement learning when results are delayed and interleaved in time. *Proc. INNC-90-PARIS*, Paris, pp. 860–63.

Myers, C. (1991) Learning with delayed reinforcement through attention-driven buffering. *Int. J. of Neural Systems*, **1** (4), 337–46.

Myers, C. (1992) A model of visual discrimination learning in Octopus vulgaris. *Journal of Intelligent Systems*, to appear.

Nguyen, D. and Widrow, B. (1989) The truck backer-upper: An example of self-learning in neural networks. *Proc. IJCNN-90-WASH, Washington*, **2**, 357–63.

Ntourntoufis, P. (1990) Self-organization properties of discriminator-based neural networks. *Proc. IJCNN-91-San Diego, San Diego*, **2**, 319–24.

O'Keefe, J. and Nadel, L. (1978) *The hippocampus as a cognitive map*, Clarendon Press, Oxford.

O'Keefe, J. (1979) A review of the hippocampal place cells. *Progress in Neurobiology*, **13**, 419–39.

Olton, D.S. (1983) Memory functions and the hippocampus, in *Neurobiology of the Hippocampus* (Ed. W. Seifert), Academic Press, London 355–73.

Parker, D. (1985) Learning logic. Technical report TR-87, Center for Computational Research in Economics and Management Science, MIT, Cambridge, MA.

Patarnello, S. and Carnevalli, P. (1990) Learning to predict the consequences of one's own actions, in *Parallel Processing in Neural systems and Computers* (Eds. R. Eckmiller, G. Hartmann, G. Hauske), Elsevier Science, Amsterdam, pp. 237–240.

Pearce, J. (1987) *Introduction to Animal Cognition*, Lawrence Erlbaum, London.

Pierrel, R. and Sherman, J. (1963) Barnabus, the rat with college training. *Brown Alumni Monthly*, February 1963, Brown University.

Rawlins, J. (1985) Associations across time: The hippocampus as a temporary memory store. *Behavioral and Brain Sciences*, **8**, 479–96.

Rescorla, R. and Wanger, A. (1972) A theory of Pavlovian conditioning: Variations in the effectiveness of reinforcement and non-reinforcement, in *Classical Conditioning: II. Current Research and Theory* (Eds. A. Black and W. Prokasy), Appleton-Century-Crofts, New York.

Rolls, E. (1989) The representation and storage of information in neural networks in the primate cerebral cortex and hippocampus, in *The Computing Neuron* (Eds. R. Durbin, C. Miall and G. Mitchison), Addison-Wesley, Wokingham, England, 125–59.

Rumelhart, D., Hinton, G. and Williams, R. (1986) Learning internal representations by error propagation, in *Parallel Distributed Processing: Explorations in the Microstructure of Cognition* (Eds. D. Rumelhart, J. McClelland), MIT Press, London, **1**, 318–62.

Rumelhart, D. and Zipser, D. (1986) Feature discovery by competitive learning, in *Parallel Distributed Processing: Explorations in the Microstructure of Cognition* (Eds. D. Rumelhart, J. McClelland), MIT Press, London, **1**, 151–93.

Saerens, M. and Soquet, A. (1989) A neural controller. *Proc 1st IEE International Conf. on Artificial Neural Networks*, London, pp. 211–15.

Samuel, A. (1963) Some studies in machine learning using the game of checkers, in *Computers and Thought* (Eds. E. Feigenbaum, J. Feldman) McGraw-Hill, New York, pp. 71–105.

Selverston, A. (1988) A consideration of invertebrate central pattern generators as computational databases. *Neural Networks*, **1**(2), 109–17.

Shapiro, J. (1989) Hard learning in boolean neural networks, in *New Developments in Neural Computing* (Eds. J. Taylor, C. Mannion), Adam Hilger, Bristol, pp. 125–32.

Shepanski, J. and Macy, S. (1988) Teaching artificial neural systems to drive: Manual training techniques for autonomous systems, in *Neural Information Processing*

Systems (Ed D. Anderson), American Institute of Physics, New York, pp. 693–700.

Squire, L. (1987) *Memory and Brain*, Oxford University Press, New York.

Stanton, P. and Sejnowski, T. (1989) Storing covariance by the associative long-term potentiation and depression of synaptic strengths in the hippocampus, in *Advances in Neural Information Processing I* (Ed D. Touretzky), Morgan Kaufman, San Mateo, CA.

Stein, J. (1987) *An Introduction to Neurophysiology*, Blackwell Scientific Publications, London.

Sutherland, N. (1957) Visual discriminations of orientation and shape by the octopus. *Nature*, **179**, 11–13.

Sutherland, R.J. and Rudy, J.W. (1989) Configural association theory: The role of the hippocampal formation in learning, memory and amnesia. *Psychobiology*, **17**(2), 129–44.

Sutton, R. (1988) Learning to predict by the methods of temporal differences. *Machine Learning*, **3**, 9–44.

Taylor, J. (1972) Spontaneous behaviour in neural networks, *J. Theoretical Biology*, **36**, 512–28.

Tesauro, G. and Sejnowski, T. (1988) A "neural" network that learns to play backgammon, in *Neural Information Processing Systems*. (Ed. D. Anderson), American Institute of Physics, New York, pp. 794–803.

Tighe, T. (1982) *Modern Learning Theory: Foundations and Fundamental Issues*, Oxford University Press, Oxford.

Walker, S. (1987) *Animal Learning: An Introduction*. Routledge and Kegan Paul, London.

Wang, J. and Grondin, R. (1989) Novel training algorithm for limited connection networks. *Proc. 1st IEE International Conference on Artificial Neural Networks*, London, pp. 387–9.

Wells, M. and Wells, J. (1957) Repeated presentation experiments and the function of vertical lobe in octopus. *J. Experimental Biology*, **34**, 378–93.

Wells, M. (1959) A touch-learning centre in Octopus. *J. Experimental Biology*, **36**, 590–612.

Wells, M. (1968) *Lower Animals*, Weidenfeld and Nicholson, London.

Werbos, P. (1974) *Beyond regression: New tools prediction and analysis in the behavioral sciences*. PhD thesis, Harvard University, Cambridge, MA.

Widrow, B. and Hoff, M. (1960) Adaptive switching circuits. *Institute of Radio Engineers, Western Electronic Show and Convention, Convention Record*, **4**, 96–194.

Widrow, B. and Smith, F. (1964) Pattern-recognizing control systems, in *Computer and Information Sciences* (J. Tou, R. Wilcox), Spartan Books, New York, pp. 288–317.

Widrow, B., Gupta, N. and Maitra, S. (1973) Punish/reward: Learning with a critic in adaptive systems. *IEEE Trans. on Systems, Man and Cybernetics*, **SMC-3**(5), 455–65.

Wong, K. and Sherrington, D. (1989) The maximum storage capacity in boolean associative memories, in *New Developments in Neural Computing* (Eds. J. Taylor, C. Mannion), Adam Hilger, Bristol, pp. 133–40.

Young, J. (1958a) Effect of removal of various amounts of vertical lobe on visual discrimination in Octopus. *Proc. Royal Society of London*, **B149**, 441–62.

Young, J. (1958b) Responses of untrained octopuses to various figures and the effect of removal of the vertical lobe. *Proc. Royal Society of London*, **B149**, 463–83.

Young, J. (1960) Unit processes in the formation of representations in the memory of Octopus. *Proc. Royal Society of London*, **B-153**, 1–17.

Young, J. (1963) *A Model of the Brain*, Clarendon Press, Oxford.

Young, J. (1968) Reversal of a visual preference in Octopus after removal of the vertical lobe. *J. Experimental Biology*, **49**, 413–19.

Young, J. (1970) Short and long memories in Octopus and the influence of the vertical lobe system. *J. Experimental Biology*, **51**, 385–93.

Young, J. (1971) *The Anatomy of the Nervous System of Octopus vulgaris*, Clarendon Press, Oxford.

Zola-Morgan, S., Squire, L. and Mishkin, M. (1982) The anatomy of amnesia: Amygdala-hippocampus versus temporal stem. *Science*, **218**, 1337–9.

Index